I0560936

The Magic of Realigning

From the Inside Out

Because you weren't meant to just

get through the day

Kassandra Hamilton

Copyright © Kassandra Hamilton 2025

All Rights Reserved

No part of this publication may be reproduced, distributed, or transmitted in any form or by any means, including photocopying, recording, or other electronic or mechanical methods, without the author's prior written permission, except in the case of brief quotations embodied in critical reviews and certain other non-commercial uses permitted by copyright law. For permission requests, please get in touch with the author.

Dedication

This book is dedicated to those who feel overwhelmed, anxious, or stuck in their lives, know deep down there must be another way to live, and are seeking more passion, purpose, and alignment with who they are meant to be.

Acknowledgments

Thank you from the bottom (and top, sides, and all around) of my heart to my team of amazing humans. I'm talking about my community, friends, sisters, brothers, family, and wise owls, the people who have taught me valuable lessons.

To those who have reflected myself back to me, providing insights, triggers, and conflicts that allowed me to learn and grow, thank you.

Thank you to my mother for showing me how to be strong and take care of myself. I am deeply grateful to the wise women in my life who offer beautiful insights and perspective shifts that help reshape the narratives I carry.

To my dear friends, Michael Dalton and David Raphael, who guided me at the beginning of my journey back to my inner self through energy work, thank you.

To my partner, for always supporting me and reminding me of my strength and commitment to my mission, I am endlessly grateful for you.

I also want to give a heartfelt shoutout to Robyn, Ara, Tamar, and Wes, who were the very first people I trusted to read my book in its early stages. Thank you for holding space for my vulnerability and for witnessing my words before they were ready for the world. Being seen in that raw, creative process was a powerful part of this journey. It was one that helped transform my writing from something private into something shared. Your presence in this process mattered more than you know.

The number of women, men, animals, creatures, and souls who have shaped my life experience is vast. If you are reading this and we have met in this lifetime, know that I appreciate you for the role you have played in my journey.

I am deeply grateful for each of you, and I absolutely love participating in this magical, frustrating, brilliant, and tenacious life we are living. What a gift!

About The Author

Kassandra is a writer dedicated to sharing stories that inspire personal development and growth. She holds a degree in Biology & International Development and a Master's in Science focused on Global Health. Her unique perspective blends data-driven insights with storytelling.

With years of experience managing health information projects with First Nations communities in Canada, Kassandra has developed a deep appreciation for the power of storytelling, especially in translating complex qualitative data into compelling narratives.

Beyond writing, she is a passionate coach and mentor for people experiencing burnout and overwhelm, guiding them back to alignment with purpose and passion in their lives.

In her spare time, Kassandra is a singer and songwriter, performing at local open mics and recording music with her partner. She also enjoys hiking with her dog, dancing, volunteering in her community, and exploring new cultures through travel.

Preface

The Magic of Realigning From the Inside Out

The term "abracadabra" is often associated with magic tricks, and that's no accident. It literally means, "With my word, I create." Words shape our reality. They *are* the magic. But where do they come from?

The answer is YOU.

Create a thought → Speak the thought → Act on the thought → Create your reality = Abracadabra. Magic.

Sit with that for a moment. We are constantly projecting what we hold inside.

Have you ever considered what words or phrases you frequently use that might be reinforcing negative patterns in your life? How might you shift your language to better align with the life you desire?

By looking at how we are operating in the world, what patterns are showing up in our life and why, and then choosing to shift our experience of reality from the inside out, we can create real magic. We can start living a life worth living full of passion, purpose, joy, and authentic connection.

It doesn't matter how old you are or what you have been through up to this point. The fact that we are alive is a miracle, and we are absolutely the magicians of our lives. In these pages, I'll share my story to show you why I know this to be true.

This book is your wand, and each chapter a spell to help you remember the magic that's always been within.

Introduction

Navigating Disconnect: The Digital Paradox

"For it's in this dance the delicate waltz between silicon and soul that we find purpose, meaning, and fulfillment"

I was 27 years old when I hit rock bottom. You wouldn't have known it from the outside. I had just moved to a big city, settled into a downtown apartment, and landed what looked like a great job. On the surface, everything looked fine. But within three months of moving, all four of my grandparents and my dog died one after the other. Not long after, my relationship fell apart, and I had a major fallout with the only friends I had in the city. My social media, though, told a different story. And that disconnect between the life I was projecting and the reality I was living is where this story begins.

Anxiety and depression are on the rise globally, and the trend is well-documented. Doctors now diagnose these conditions more frequently than ever before. Among the many contributing factors, technology has emerged as a major amplifier: constant notifications, blue-lit screens, and endless doom-scrolling all take a toll. As we move through headlines filled with crisis, climate change, political conflict, and pandemics that have physically and emotionally distanced us, our mental health is increasingly strained. The full impact is only beginning to surface, but one truth is clear: as external crises intensify, our inner worlds mirror that chaos.

Today, the pressure is even greater. Economic instability, political division, and the looming reality of AI add new layers to our collective anxiety. What once belonged to science fiction is now part of daily life. As we race to explore these technological frontiers or dream of colonizing Mars, as some billionaires suggest, we're faced with a hard truth: no amount of escape, innovation, or digital sophistication will solve the deeper issues we carry within. These so-called "escape routes" remain fantasies for the privileged few, offering the illusion of a "best life" while most of us are left here, on Earth, navigating a complex and uncertain reality.

Humans are hardwired for connection. And yet, in this age of constant virtual connectivity, we feel more isolated than ever. I call this the digital paradox. Despite the convenience of always being connected, true human connection has become increasingly rare. If you've ever looked up in a public place, a coffee shop, a bus, or a waiting room, you've probably noticed how everyone is glued to their phones. Someone once asked me if I thought humans would eventually evolve into hybrids of flesh and machine. Watching our behavior today, I realize that, in some ways, we already have.

The Inside Out Approach

In the pages that follow, I invite you to flip the narrative. Instead of looking outward for answers, we begin to live from the inside out. This book is an invitation to pause, to reflect on your own path through this chaotic world, and to rediscover what happens when we reclaim authentic connection with ourselves and with others. I encourage you to engage with the questions and exercises throughout the book. Write your reflections. Try the tools and techniques. Let them ground you, and take the time to integrate what arises.

Beyond the screens and carefully curated feeds, a richer, more meaningful human experience is waiting. One conscious choice at a time, we can begin to weave authenticity, connection, and purpose back into our lives and live with greater passion and intention.

In the midst of collective anxiety, I've found a lifeline; a practice that offers a way through. The tools I share here are not about escaping the chaos of our modern world, they are designed to help you find your unique place within a landscape shaped by political, environmental, and technological upheaval. They are invitations to become the magician of your own life.

These reflections, stories, and strategies have supported me on my own path. I offer them not as linear solutions or quick fixes, but as part of a lifelong commitment to living authentically. And this isn't a one-time effort. It's an ongoing practice; a lifelong exploration of what it means to stay human in a world that constantly pulls us away from ourselves.

Let me ask you: Have you ever allowed yourself to truly imagine the life you want to create? Or are you stuck in survival mode, burnt out, exhausted, and wondering what it's all for? Or maybe you're in a job you once thought would fulfill you, only to realize: this isn't it.

If you could wave a magic wand, what would you really want? What if I told you there was a way to step out of crisis mode and into alignment with your true desires? Would you have the courage to explore it?

I know from personal experience that it's possible to create a life filled with meaning and genuine inner happiness. But it starts with asking one simple, powerful question:

If not now, then when?

This journey unfolds in four steps:

1. Observe what's unfolding around you.
2. Recognize how external forces are impacting your inner world.
3. Refocus inward and retune your mind, body, and spirit.
4. Live from the inside out with passion, purpose, and authenticity.

You can live authentically for yourself and for others. The societal blueprint we've inherited doesn't lead to true freedom. But you have the power to redesign your path and create the life you were meant to live.

Part 1

Observing Our Outer World

Chapter 1

Authentic Connection

"We risk becoming passive participants in a world where the very technology designed to serve us ends up shaping and often fragmenting our inner lives."

Social media platforms invite us to broadcast our highlights: sun-soaked vacations, gourmet meals, laughter-filled gatherings. But what about the shadows? The messy, imperfect moments, the heartaches, the self-doubt are hidden from view. We've become great masters at curating our "best lives," trading authenticity for illusion.

This culture of falsity on social media only amplified the anxiety and depression I was experiencing at age 27 at the time I hit rock bottom.

The shift toward a filtered, curated reality is deeply unsettling. When I see people glued to their screens, avoiding eye contact, and disengaged from the present moment, I can't help but think: no wonder anxiety is at an all-time high. Disconnection from the present weakens relationships and erodes our capacity for genuine connection. Beneath the surface of our hyper-connected digital landscape, a quiet isolation festers, fueling the very internal crises we seek to escape.

Authentic connection begins when we remember the magic of being seen fully, vulnerably, and without masks.

I've lost friends over this. After expressing to one friend that I often felt unimportant when we met in person because she was always on her phone, I decided to give it one last try. We hadn't seen each other in about six months, so we agreed to each drive over an hour to meet halfway at a coffee shop.

We spent an hour together, and for forty-five of those sixty minutes, she was on her phone. This wasn't the first time, but it was the last. I realized I wanted a deeper, in-person connection in my friendships, and this particular friendship no longer offered that.

The documentary *The Social Dilemma* (2020) sheds light on how social media platforms affect our mental health, privacy, and society at large. Former employees of major tech companies like Facebook, Google, and Twitter reveal how these platforms are deliberately engineered to exploit human psychology, keeping us hooked and often leading us into addictive behaviors.

Algorithms hijack our attention, spread misinformation, polarize opinions, and amplify a sense of perpetual inadequacy. Without mindfulness, we risk becoming passive participants, and allow the very technology designed to serve us to shape and fragment our inner lives.

But I'm here to tell you: there's a better, more fulfilling way forward. It begins with slowing down and honestly exploring what's happening inside you, getting clear on where you are, what you need, and where stronger, more meaningful sources of connection can be found. From that space, real transformation is possible.

Technology is here to stay, continuing to shape our future and deliver a constant stream of "doom stories" from across the globe. But when it comes to our relationships, both with ourselves and others, it can only take us so far. No matter how advanced our digital tools become, they cannot fill the void if we're not at peace within ourselves.

In a world bombarded by external influences, ads, endless scrolling, and pressure to conform to polished ideals, loneliness quietly creeps in, leaving many of us feeling disconnected and dissatisfied. As the world becomes more chaotic and uncertain, and as anxiety rises alongside it, we are swept into a powerful current of change and confusion.

The truth is, digital connections lack real depth. Emojis can't replace meaningful conversations. Virtual "likes" don't stand in for genuine affirmation. So, how do we express and embrace our true selves, the big, messy, imperfect parts of who we are?

These are the questions I began asking myself, the same questions that ultimately gave birth to this book. I believe the answer lies in creating spaces where we can show up as our authentic selves, without filters or pretense. We can reclaim our lives from autopilot not by rejecting technology or resisting change, but by finding our own unique balance within it all.

It's in the delicate dance between binary code and beating heart that we rediscover meaning, purpose, and fulfillment.

Here's what I know now: while it may not be immediately obvious, the moment you choose to live differently to carve your own path, to find clarity amid the noise through conscious awareness, your entire world can begin to shift.

My mission is simple: to walk alongside others on the journey toward authenticity and expression, to help uncover the courage to be happy, and to create positive ripple effects in the world. I want to support you in remembering why you're here on this planet and to start living on purpose.

It's up to each of us to listen to the quiet strength within and, in doing so, to find or regain passion, purpose, and fulfillment.

Yes, you can live the life you dream about.

Chapter 2

Changing My Relationship with Anxiety:

A Personal Story

"Anxiety is merely a messenger and can help to shape our journey by indicating what needs to be nourished in our inner world."

Roots of Anxiety

For over two decades, anxiety and perfectionism were powerful forces in my life. But it wasn't until university that I truly understood how tightly they had taken hold of me. The pressure to meet impossibly high standards, always striving for more, never feeling like I was enough, left me emotionally drained. No matter how much I achieved, I was left with exhaustion, overwhelm, and a deep sense of unworthiness and guilt.

My identity became inextricably tied to my productivity. If I wasn't producing, guilt would consume me. These feelings of inadequacy only fueled my anxiety, creating a relentless feedback loop that felt impossible to break. But how did I get there? Let me take you back to the beginning.

When I Discovered My Passion

When I was thirteen, my mom took my brother and me to India for a year to immerse ourselves in a different culture. At that young age, I was catapulted into a world far removed from the comfort and familiarity of home.

In India, I witnessed suffering on a scale I had never imagined. The streets were filled with people suffering from conditions like leprosy, scurvy, and malnutrition, diseases that modern medicine can often prevent or treat. Despite global medical advancements, these illnesses remained widespread and largely ignored.

What I saw deeply upset me. I felt a profound sense of injustice that carved a permanent place in my heart. When I returned home, I was determined to dedicate my life to addressing health disparities between the developed and developing worlds. I felt driven by a passion to help build a more equitable world.

But coming back to Canada was harder than I expected.

The friends I had left behind seemed unaware of the magnitude of what I had experienced. Questions like "Did you get a tan in India?" or "Was the curry spicy?" felt trivial, even insulting, in contrast to the harsh realities I had witnessed. As a result, I withdrew into myself. I fell into a depression, disconnected from those around me, and poured all my energy into my studies, counting the days until graduation.

Looking back, I realize few people understood how deeply I was struggling.

Academic Overdrive

After high school, I spent a year traveling and teaching in Thailand. When I returned, my commitment to global health equity was stronger than ever. After some reflection, I enrolled in an undergraduate program in biology and international development.

But academia only intensified my anxiety and perfectionism. I pushed myself harder and harder, striving for excellence while falling apart inside. I became consumed by obsessive behaviors: checking locks repeatedly, rereading my assignments endlessly, and losing sleep over the smallest decisions. What began as coping mechanisms for uncertainty quickly spiraled into something darker.

I would check the stove six times before bed. I held my hands under the faucet to make sure every drop of water was gone over and over again. What started as a need for control evolved into full-blown OCD. My demand for order and perfection became all-consuming, leaving me mentally exhausted and socially isolated.

With the help of counseling, I completed my degree. But by the time I graduated, I was burned out, disillusioned with the academic system, and unsure of what to do next. The thought of pursuing more education felt unbearable.

And yet, beneath the fatigue, a quiet curiosity about the world began to reawaken.

At one point during my studies, I had envisioned a future in medical school. But the idea of balancing such a demanding path with my fragile mental health felt overwhelming. I took the MCAT and quickly realized that this path wasn't for me. I soon recognized that Western medicine's focus on physical symptoms, often without attention to mental, emotional, or spiritual well-being, didn't align with what I had witnessed abroad.

Passion Ignited

My experiences overseas have shown me the importance of serving people in a more holistic way, addressing the full spectrum of well-being. Reflecting on these insights, I began questioning the entire approach to health in the Western world.

(Yes, I question things a lot.)

I also thought back to an elective I had taken on environmental racism, which examined the disproportionate impact of toxic waste on marginalized communities. Why weren't we applying the same lens of justice and intersectionality to healthcare? That question became the spark that led me to pursue a Master of Science in Global Health, momentarily quieting the anxiety that had once held me back.

My passion for making a difference was strong. As my studies continued, I also learned coping techniques for anxiety, such as meditation and therapy. These tools helped me complete the program, and by the time I graduated, I was ready to step into the workforce armed with knowledge, purpose, and a deep desire to make a meaningful impact.

However, reality had other plans.

Spinning Wheels

Despite sending out over two hundred job applications, I faced endless rejection even for entry-level roles like pharmacy assistant, for which I was vastly overqualified. It wasn't just about the jobs themselves; it felt like the culmination of years of striving. My confidence began to slip.

I started to wonder if all my education and lived experiences had led me down a path that was ultimately empty. I had done everything "right" and still couldn't catch a break. Feeling deflated, I returned to bartending, questioning whether I had taken the wrong road altogether.

I felt lost.

Nearly a year later, a small breakthrough came: a clinical research assistant position opened up. It was only tangentially related to my field and barely paid enough to cover rent, but I took it. I would be running a small clinic on my own. In hindsight, I should have negotiated for a better salary and title, but desperation spoke louder than confidence.

Once again, I packed my belongings and moved to a small, dusty town six hours away from everything familiar. The job's future was anything but certain. The company's director warned me that unless I turned things around quickly, the entire research operation could collapse.

No pressure, right?

Each day, I walked into work wondering if I'd walk out unemployed. The company's position was precarious, and my anxiety gnawed at me daily. Still, I stuck it out, knowing I had to keep moving forward, even if I was hanging on by a thread both to my job and my mental health.

Let's just say I was always on the lookout for the next opportunity.

About a year later, I finally landed what I thought was my dream job: a government role in Vancouver focused on quality improvement in patient care. On paper, it was everything I had worked toward: it felt like the long-awaited alignment of my mission to bridge gaps in healthcare. And it was professional, stable, and well-paying.

Hallelujah.

But soon after moving, everything began to unravel.

Breakdown and Burnout Again

My living situation turned toxic. My roommates were disruptive, and within three months, I had to move out. I ended up in a tiny, cramped apartment alone, gradually losing contact with the only people I knew in the city.

Then came a series of personal losses. My long-distance boyfriend and I broke up. My family's dog passed away. And within weeks, I lost both of my grandmothers and my paternal grandfather.

To say that grief overwhelmed me is an understatement.

Anxiety returned with a vengeance this time, nearly paralyzing and I withdrew from everyone. I felt more anxious, more isolated, and more heartbroken than I ever had before.

I felt like a vulnerable prisoner to my emotions: unprotected, unsafe. Alone.

My world was falling apart, and I had no control. Inside, I felt like I was on fire, knotted, tangled, confused, while simultaneously being swallowed by a black hole. The pain was both chaotic and hollow and I didn't think I'd be able to climb out.

Fueling the Fire – Social Media

Around this time, social media began to take a firmer hold on the public's attention, especially for those with access to smartphones. Platforms like TikTok, Facebook, and Instagram became deeply ingrained in daily life. As I spent more time online, I found myself constantly comparing my reality to the polished images on my feed.

I couldn't help but wonder why my life didn't match the seemingly perfect ones others portrayed, even though, deep down, I knew those were only curated snapshots.

Still, the comparisons fed my sense of inadequacy, deepening my sadness, disconnection, and an aching sense of aloneness. Over time, I became increasingly isolated not just from others, but from myself. In the midst of it all, I fell into depression.

What Lies Behind Social Media

Social media, in many ways, mirrors what Adlerian psychology calls the inferiority complex. According to this theory, all human problems stem from interpersonal relationships: we are constantly comparing ourselves to others. This concept is explored in the book *The Courage to Be Disliked*; without comparison, there would be no internal competition. But within that competition, inferiority is born.

Social media thrives on this dynamic, magnifying self-doubt and the illusion that we are somehow not enough.

It's no surprise that most people don't share the raw, unfiltered details of their lives. I certainly didn't feel inspired to share the breakdown I was experiencing. My struggles didn't measure up to the curated, idealized content we're constantly exposed to.

And so, the disconnection deepened first from others, but more importantly, from myself. We're encouraged to present a version of life that isn't entirely authentic. And while I appeared to be doing well, living downtown with a promising career, I felt more lost than ever.

It was a deeply unsettling experience.

The truth was, the image I projected online was completely disconnected from how I felt inside. The paradox was painful: my carefully curated posts suggested I had everything together when, in reality, I felt like I was falling apart.

In search of support, I turned to grief counseling. During those sessions, I came to a profound realization: I wasn't just grieving the loss of my loved ones. I was mourning the life I had built, the one shaped more by external expectations than by my own true desires.

I had followed all the "right" steps: academic achievement, career progression, financial independence. But something essential was missing. Despite everything I had worked for, a persistent emptiness remained, and I could no longer ignore it.

The Tipping Point

Eventually, my body started to sound the alarm.

I felt panic-stricken, tense, and paralyzed even by minor discomforts. I was locked in a near-constant fight-or-flight state. I wasn't happy in my government job, where much of the work felt performative rather than impactful. Social media felt fake. I felt hopeless and helpless.

I knew I couldn't go on like this.

Anxiety was no longer just a response to stressors; it had become a deep, internal reckoning. A massive, undeniable call for change. I couldn't push it down anymore.

One evening, I collapsed onto the floor of my 400-square-foot apartment. On my knees, hands pressed to the ground, I wept uncontrollably. I began begging, pleading with anything or anyone to give me a sign, some kind of guidance.

"If I've done everything *right*, then why am I so anxious and unfulfilled?" I cried.

"Why does it feel like there's a void inside me?"

"Is this really all there is?"

It was the same feeling I'd had when I considered medical school. The same ache I felt after completing my master's degree. Despite following my passion, I kept finding myself trapped in a societal structure that didn't allow me to pursue it authentically.

I wanted more.

Something deeper.

Something that mattered.

I kept asking myself: What was all this for?

I wanted my life to mean something more than just working a 9–5, going to the gym, and having two weeks of vacation each year. Deep down, I knew there had to be a better way to live. A more fulfilling way to contribute to the world. I wanted to believe there were others out there who craved the same kind of depth and meaning I longed for.

Do you ever feel that, too?

Healing Begins – The Inside Out Approach is Born

After that pivotal moment, I began to slow down.

I started an internal inquiry, asking myself the questions I had long avoided: Who am I, really? Who am I outside of social media, outside of my career, outside of other people's expectations? Who am I when I'm alone with myself?

For the first time in years, I allowed myself to sit in silence; long, uninterrupted silence. I lit candles. I meditated. I explored alternative healing practices, opening myself to anything new or different from the approach I had followed up to that point.

Through counseling and deep personal reflection, I came to a profound realization: true self-satisfaction comes from within, not from external achievements or validation.

As I write this, I can hear the voice of skepticism, even in myself: *Well, yeah, that makes sense.* And intellectually, it does. But in practice, so many of us, myself included, have been conditioned to look outside ourselves for direction. We strive to meet societal expectations and validation, check every box, and then wonder why we still feel unhappy or unfulfilled.

Have you ever experienced this?

Anxiety as a Messenger

What I discovered next surprised me. Anxiety wasn't my enemy; it was a messenger. A wise, insistent voice pointing me toward what needed healing. The louder it became, the more urgently it demanded my attention.

I began to see emotions as a child. They don't want to be fixed or silenced. They want to be seen, heard, and acknowledged. The more I ignored my anxiety, the louder it became. But when I slowed down and truly listened, I understood what it was trying to tell me.

The anxiety was never random. It was a signal. A call to come back to myself. To stop running, stop shaming, stop escaping, and instead, be present. I realized I had spent so much time trying to outrun my discomfort that I'd lost the connection I so deeply yearned for.

And that connection? It had to begin within me.

Meeting My Mentor

Around this time, I met a mentor, David Raphael, who introduced me to the idea of energetic awareness, specifically, becoming conscious of where I was leaking my energy and how to reclaim it.

Through the process of slowing down, David helped me realize something powerful: the peace, the passion, and the authentic purpose I had been desperately chasing were not outside of me. They had always been within me.

He introduced me to energy healing, and my entire world began to open.

I'll admit, I was skeptical at first. But I remember one session vividly. He asked me to close my eyes, tune into my own energy system, and led me through a visualization where I began to gently direct its flow and state. What happened next was unlike anything I had experienced.

My body felt weightless, like it was floating. For the first time in a long while, I wasn't anxious. I wasn't panicking. I was completely at peace, grounded in presence with myself. Time seemed to disappear, and all I could hear was the steady rhythm of my own heartbeat.

It was in that moment that I realized how much I had been neglecting my inner world in pursuit of my goals. I had spent years focusing on the destination without checking in on the traveler.

And that traveler was exhausted, overwhelmed, and yearning for something deeper.

Slowly, I began to shift from doing to being. In that shift, I found a sense of peace I had long been searching for. This marked the beginning of a new chapter, one where I started to reclaim my inner power and free myself.

This is when I started creating the inside-out approach. I began to flip the narrative I had carried for so long, that if I achieved, I would be happy. What I really needed to learn was who I was on the inside, stripped away from the goals and achievements, perfectionism, and filters.

Turns out, the peace and happiness I could claim by starting from this place were immeasurable.

By sharing my story, I hope you find the courage to listen to your own inner voice, trust your intuitive path, and discover the strength that has always been within you. Or, at the very least, to begin getting curious.

A New Way Forward

Today, I have a phrase written on my wall as a daily prompt to stay present: *"I am a human being, not a human doing."* The thing is, life happens in the moment. If we are too focused on chasing the next goal or achievement, we miss it.

Anxiety still visits me, but it no longer controls me. I have learned to coexist with it to let it guide me rather than define me. I've learned to listen to my feelings, especially the discomfort I once tried so hard to outrun.

The more I embraced those feelings, the more my anxiety began to fade. The more I am connected to myself. The more I have agency over my life.

I now see anxiety as one of my messengers, helping to shape my journey by indicating where my inner world needs nourishment. Through presence and stillness, I believe we all have the power to listen to our own inner guide, and that this is where we begin to shape our lives from within.

Anxiety is an ally if we learn how to reframe our relationship with it.

Each moment I chose presence over panic, I reclaimed a little more of my power, like gathering pieces of a forgotten spell.

It was the beginning of a new alchemy: transforming fear into clarity.

Are you willing to try this on for yourself?

In the next chapter, we'll explore a crucial topic in learning how to live from the inside out: *control.*

Part 2

Understanding

Chapter 3

Control and Surrender:

A Mindful Journey of Letting Go

"Surrender is not defeat; it is liberation. A hidden portal to trust.
It is a cosmic handshake between self and universe."

The Illusion of Control

For much of my life, control felt like the only way to stay safe. If I could predict every possible outcome, I thought I could protect myself from pain. Anxiety would whisper in my ear that control was the only way to feel safe. It insisted that if I could master my circumstances, hold tightly to my routines, micromanage my environment, and predict every outcome, I could find peace. But ironically, the harder I gripped, the more I strangled my peace.

Deepak Chopra once said that when we cling to a moment, we suffocate it, and this has really stuck with me.

Have you ever clung so tightly to an outcome, relationship, or idea of yourself that it ended up becoming heavy and suffocating? Over the years, I have learned this the hard way through struggle, heartache, and ultimately, a deep dive into my own fears. In the process, I learned that no matter how hard I tried to orchestrate life, there would always be forces beyond my grasp, such as loss, change, and other people's choices. Clinging to control doesn't prevent pain; it often amplifies it. It wasn't until I learned to lighten up on control and move through the fear that I truly began to feel what it's like to experience liberation. This is a foundational idea to unpack and understand as we learn how to live from the inside out.

Where Control Began – The Pivotal Moment

One memory stands out more than others. When I trace the origins of my need for control, it always brings me back to this moment.

I was eight years old and had gone into the garage to get something. I was in a rush, and in my haste, I forgot to lock the garage door afterward. At the time, our neighborhood had a reputation for break-ins, and my mother had repeatedly told me to be extra cautious. She had warned me to make sure I locked the garage every time I went in, especially since she had an expensive road bike stored there. Growing up, we were not wealthy, so that bike was one of the few valuable things my mom owned.

The next morning, I discovered both the backyard gate and the garage door open, and my mother's bike was gone.

The guilt hit me hard. I had failed. My careless mistake, though small in the grand scheme of things, felt like an irreparable crack I couldn't fix. For the next two years, for whatever reason, that moment stayed with me, heavy in my chest. I could not escape the haunting image of that open gate.

Every night, I would lie in bed, staring at the backyard gate through my window, ready and waiting for anyone or anything to break in. I felt like I had to prove myself somehow and make my wrongs right. I was extremely hard on myself, beating myself up internally for making such a colossal mistake. The guilt was overwhelming.

As a child, I had little agency over the external circumstances that affected my life. My mother shared with me when I was nine years old that she had been abused as a child and didn't grow up in a safe environment. I didn't realize it at the time, but looking back, the message I internalized was that women needed to protect themselves. And control is a perfect way for our psyche to do this. Additionally, my mom's abusive upbringing and lack of receiving love from her parents resulted in her being loving toward me one moment and withdrawing when she felt triggered by something. I internalized a message that love was conditional and could be taken away at a moment's notice. Emotional instability amplified during my parents' divorce when I turned twelve. It provoked an already precarious sense of emotional safety and left me grappling with a new, unsettling reality.

Without even realizing it, I started trying to control everything around me to regain some sense of order. I had this intense need to protect myself and feel safe in order to feel okay.

How Control Has Functioned in My Life (and Failed)

My behaviors began to change from these experiences. I became obsessed with locking doors, checking stoves, and monitoring every little detail around me. Over time, my mind grew rigid. My thinking got divided into right and wrong, black and white. Always seeking stability, my mind began to latch onto control as the only source of security. I became obsessed with organizing every detail of my world.

I wasn't just managing my environment anymore; I was really trying to control it. If I could control my surroundings, maybe, just maybe, I could protect myself from further pain, disappointment, guilt, or shame. If I tried to manage everything: my schoolwork, my environment, my relationships, then perhaps I could prevent any more emotional upheaval. It was an attempt to soothe the deep, unseen wounds inside me.

As I grew older, I extended my need for control to others. I tried to shape their actions, hoping that by influencing those around me, I could maintain some semblance of safety. Safety became my number one priority. But no matter how tightly I gripped, the unease remained. Control did not bring peace; it only deepened my anxiety and made the people around me increasingly annoyed.

I shrugged it off for a while, thinking it was just part of my "Type A" personality. Deep down, though, I wondered why I was behaving this way.

Through countless conversations, self-reflection, and therapy, I began to uncover the roots of my intense need for control. It wasn't just a personality trait or random behavior; it was a defense mechanism born from a deep-seated fear of not being safe in the world.

I finally realized that no matter how much I tried to control the world around me, I was still wrestling with an inner part of me I couldn't seem to tame. And in this constant striving for control, I disconnected from the present moment. From life itself.

The Paradox of Control & the Start of Letting Go

The more I tried to control, the more I set myself up for disappointment. This paradox became clearer as I got older and began to confront conflict in my relationships. When things didn't go according to plan, I became frustrated, resentful, and anxious. And those around me, especially past boyfriends, often felt they were failing to meet my expectations.

Over time, I started to realize I was not only taking on the burden of trying to fix or control others, but I was also robbing them of the opportunity to have their own life experience.

Worse still, I lost the ability to enjoy the simple, spontaneous moments of life. I had become so focused on making sure everything was "right" and that I felt "safe" that I no longer allowed myself the freedom to experience life as it came.

For years, I had clung to life, trying to force it into neat categories. In doing so, I suffocated the essence of being present and took myself out of the opportunity to notice magic unfolding all around me. I thought I was protecting myself. But by controlling everything and managing life as a series of tasks, I was denying myself the vulnerability needed to flow with life to be open, to grow trust in my relationships, and to live fully.

It feels so heavy to carry around this type of resistance.

The Turning Point – Surrender

Though painful, this realization marked a turning point when I was 30 years old. I began to question my relationship with control, where it came from, why I clung to it, and whether it truly served me.

The more I explored, the more I understood that my need for control was rooted in childhood fears: fear of failure, uncertainty, vulnerability, and a loss of safety. While it felt familiar, over time, this illusion became ironically heavy and suffocating.

I wanted to grow and move forward in my life, so I kept telling myself, "I am safe to be vulnerable," knowing full well that change requires vulnerability. But something still didn't resonate. It felt forced, and the heaviness remained.

Something was still off.

So I began mentally excavating to understand what was truly happening beneath the surface.

Let me give you an example; one you can try for yourself.

I realized that the problem wasn't lack of control, it was my fear of what might happen if I let go. So I asked myself:

What's the worst that could happen if I let go?

What if I eased that grip and trusted that life would unfold as it should, even without a plan for every detail?

At first, this felt terrifying. But I kept going.

My first answer was, "If I let go, I will be giving up my safety and protection."

Then I asked, "What's the worst part of that?"

My answer: "I will be left vulnerable."

I pressed further: "What's the worst part of that?"

And I answered, "I could be hurt or put in a position of pain."

Finally, I thought, "Maybe I could die."

But something in my mind said, "Wait a second, you won't die."

Because when you're in pain and discomfort, that's when you begin to grow. That's when you build resilience, deepen awareness, and develop strength.

And with that realization, I saw the irony: the worst-case scenario buried beneath all that fear was exactly what I wanted most: growth, strength, and liberation.

This was an *aha* moment.

By clinging to control, I was preventing myself from growing and learning.

Huh.

From that insight, I realized the only way to live the fullest, most growth-oriented life was to embrace the discomfort of holding space for it and to move through to the other side of vulnerability.

Please try this series of "What's the worst that could happen?" questions to excavate your own deeper truths.

Here's another exercise you can try:

1. Notice when you're clinging to control

2. Pay attention to tightness in your chest, shallow breathing, or racing thoughts.

3. Pause and ask: *What am I afraid will happen if I let go?*

4. Take one conscious breath. Inhale deeply. Exhale slowly.

5. Remind yourself: *I am safe in this moment.*

6. Loosen your grip. See what unfolds.

If you're struggling with a sense of heaviness around control, or if you find yourself constantly managing everything down to the last detail, I believe this process might surprise and possibly free you. At the very least, it can promote a powerful shift in perspective.

There's a delicate balance between guidance and surrender, between action and trust. Letting go of control doesn't mean abandoning responsibility; it means releasing the need to force everything into place and allowing life to surprise us. It's about letting the power of life work through us, not just from us. It's about holding discomfort with the desire to grow.

Once the concept of letting go began to truly land for me, I started to experiment with it inch by inch.

Slowly, I learned and integrated into my life the understanding that control is not the key to safety. I came to realize that true security doesn't come from manipulating the world around us, but from trusting ourselves to navigate whatever comes our way.

It can be hard to look at ourselves in the mirror and confront the controlling tendencies that have shaped us. But in doing so, we begin to free ourselves. We begin to let go of outdated habits and behaviors, and in the process, we reclaim our power.

This is the second stage of learning to live from the inside out. I call it the *understanding* phase, the stage that follows the initial practice of observing what's happening around us.

This is the stage where we begin to understand how we respond to what's happening in our external environment, where we observe ourselves in the world.

Surrender isn't about giving up. It's about opening up to the possibility of a new approach. It's about releasing patterns that may have been formed at a young age but no longer support love, freedom, or growth.

So, I invite you to pause and reflect:

What are you holding on to so tightly that it's slipping through your fingers? What would happen if you let go just a little?

The very act of releasing might be the key to discovering your true strength.

My Surrender Moment – The Power of Letting Go

After years of living alone, I moved to Vancouver and lived in a house with eight other roommates. It was a dynamic, eclectic group, each of us on a path of self-discovery and healing.

Together, we began to peel back the layers of our behaviors, habits, and patterns. We worked through the subconscious beliefs that had kept us stuck for so long.

I wanted to grow as a human being and I wanted to experience what it meant to let go and surrender. I have always been deeply motivated to become the best version of myself, not just for me, but to be of service to the world and to my future children. And I knew my need for control was getting in the way.

During this time in my life, I began to confront my controlling tendencies head-on. I recognized that they stemmed from deep-seated fears I no longer needed to carry.

My roommates and I decided to host a ceremony centered around the idea of letting go. It was a space for us to collectively release our attachment to old patterns and invite something new into our lives.

The thought of letting go of control felt risky and very vulnerable. I was terrified of losing control and of what might happen if I stepped into the unknown. And yet, it was exactly that unknown I needed to confront. I knew that if I truly wanted to release my need for control, this might be the perfect opportunity.

There's something deeply profound about coming together in a sacred space to witness one another's growth, to release what no longer serves us, and to celebrate the path ahead.

This particular ceremony included plant medicine, which, when used intentionally, can be a powerful tool for deepening self-awareness and promoting emotional healing. Dr. Gabor Maté, a well-known physician and author, has written extensively about the healing power of plant-based medicines. I found myself drawn to explore this path—the idea of giving up my grip on reality felt both terrifying and strangely compelling.

About an hour before the gathering, I had a panic attack. Anxiety had gripped my throat. I became scared of what I had committed to, and I nearly backed out. My shakiness and uncertainty bubbled to the surface, and the two facilitators, as they finished setting up the space, took notice. They came over to me, gently offering to hold my hand literally through the process. They reminded me why I had chosen this path and reassured me that I didn't have to go through with it unless it truly felt right. With their support, alongside both excitement and trepidation, I stepped into ceremony.

I kept repeating to myself, "I have the courage to move through this. I want to break free."

As the medicine began to take effect and sensations shifted within my body, my instinct was to hold on to steer the ship. Panic started to rise again. I could feel it building, as if my body was fighting to maintain control. But no matter how tightly I gripped, I realized I couldn't direct the experience.

Irony, again.

My anxiety skyrocketed. The panic I had spent years suppressing rose up like a tidal wave, and I felt myself beginning to spiral. "Shit," I thought. "This is it. I can't run away from this now."

Just as I teetered on the edge of a full-blown panic attack, a quiet voice inside me, calm and reassuring, whispered:

Let go.

So I did.

I exhaled.

And with that breath, I watched myself soften and relax into the experience. My grip loosened. I unfolded.

The Change – Letting Go

As I let go, a profound shift began to take place. When I allowed myself to dissolve into the experience, I felt a deep sense of connection. A wave of relaxation washed over me. The boundaries between myself and the world blurred. Time seemed to slow. The rush of thoughts stilled, and I was no longer fighting the current in my mind. I was flowing with it. My body, spirit, and mind all felt present and connected.

I was floating.

And then, a surprising feeling: joy.

A profound, quiet joy.

And with it came a deeper knowing that everything was already okay, with or without my constant intervening.

What followed was a kaleidoscope of emotions, memories, and visions. I experienced an overwhelming sense of clarity and simplicity. I even started to laugh out loud, startled by how incredibly simple and astoundingly clear it all was. This truth I had been chasing for years suddenly sat right in front of me:

There was nothing to control.

There was only the present moment.

And that moment right there felt completely, utterly free.

It was a new feeling, and one I wanted to remember.

Life Since Understanding Surrender

Since that moment, I've understood that the true meaning of surrender isn't defeat, as many understand it to be. It's actually liberation.

I didn't have to keep carrying what I had been carrying. It was an old story, heavy and outdated, that no longer served me. I've carried the essence of surrender with me ever since. As with anything, control does slip back in, and it's an ongoing practice of remembering the feeling of letting go. Also, surrender doesn't mean abandoning my responsibilities or giving up on my goals. It means releasing the need to control every outcome, every detail. It means letting go of the urge to force everything into place.

Let's face it, life moves on its own, whether we try to control it or not. I have the ability and the sovereignty to choose. And so do you.

I'm not offering a prescription here for how you should experience surrender. I'm simply sharing the exact moment when I finally got it, when I realized I could move through life with trust in myself and in life itself. I came to understand that I am capable of navigating whatever comes my way. And so are you.

I still wrestle with the urge to control, especially in my relationship with my partner. A lifetime of feeling the need to protect myself from men and from the world doesn't vanish overnight. It's easy to slip back into old patterns, like seeing my partner's chaos as something I need to fix or organize so that I can feel safe.

But the more I let go of trying to control him, the more I see that our connection doesn't come from fixing each other. It comes from loving each other, flaws and all. The more I trust and let go, the lighter I feel.

When I catch myself falling into control, I pause. I remind myself: *This is a protection mechanism that no longer serves me.* I breathe. I let it go. I don't need to armor myself. Instead, I am choosing to hold my fear with tenderness as I step forward. Each time I release control and practice consciously letting go, I create space for myself and for the bond with my partner to deepen.

In that space of shared presence and adoration, the old stories fade and the fears soften.

We all need more love, not less. And as my partner often reminds me, love is a choice.

Here's something I invite you to try: the next time you feel the urge to control a situation or a person, try repeating this mantra:

I choose trust over control. I choose love over fear. My fear is just a story trying to protect me, and as I step forward, I release this fear with love.

The Practice of Surrender

The practice of surrender has transformed and continues to transform not only my relationship but also my work and my inner world. As I continue learning to let go, I find deeper peace and greater freedom.

That doesn't mean I never slip. I still need reminders. But I know how to return to a place of calm and I know that I don't have to control everything to be okay.

And here's the truth: being okay isn't the point.

Because I'm not always okay, none of us are.

What matters is how we respond when we're not okay. That's the heart of growth. With awareness of how I've used control to feel safe, I can now shift how I operate. I notice when I'm slipping into old habits, and I choose differently. Awareness gives us power. And action gives us change.

Life after Learning to Surrender

And so, the journey continues.

Letting go of control is a daily practice. It's found in the small moments of release, in accepting that not everything can be planned, predicted, or managed. It's in recognizing how you operate when fear arises and questioning the stories you tell yourself in that moment. Can you observe them without attaching yourself or your emotions to them? It's about getting quiet so you can really tap into the stories that you are telling yourself.

This is the "understanding" phase of living from the inside out. We start to observe ourselves with honesty and compassion. We begin to let go of the old narratives that shame or limit us. We allow the present moment to be enough without trying to fix or manipulate it.

I invite you to pause and ask yourself:

What if I trusted the process of life a little more today? What if I trusted myself a little more? What would that feel like in my body? What would it be like if this situation weren't good or bad, but just... is?

Close your eyes. Breathe into it.

In the moments where I am judging something as "bad" or a moment of "crisis," looking back, I see that those situations allowed for growth in me. The most magical moments have unfolded in surrender: chance encounters, unexpected opportunities, quiet inner peace. Through personal experience, I've come to believe that surrender is the real flex. It's a powerful act of trust in yourself, in the world, and in the divine rhythm of life. And the peace you've been seeking? It might already be within you, just waiting to be allowed in.

This process is foundational to living from the inside out. Once we understand how we operate and why, we can choose what kind of operating system we want to run on. Instead of defaulting to reaction and control, we begin to act from awareness and alignment. It's no longer autopilot. This is how we start to create the life we want.

Now that we've explored the power of letting go, I want to take you into the next concept: energy and how it moves within, around, and between us.

Chapter 4

The Dance of Energy:
From Biology to Bio-Energy Healing

"True healing requires a holistic approach, addressing the
mind, body, and spirit as an interconnected whole."

Everything Is Energy and Energy Is Everything

As a child, I had an intuitive sense that there was more to life than meets the eye. I often had vivid dreams where I stood in front of someone, healing them with my hands, alleviating pain with just a touch. Sometimes, I wouldn't even make physical contact. I would simply hold my hands near them and envision a white light flowing between us. I can only assume this was some form of energy.

As I grew older, I didn't know how to relate these dreams to the practical world. They felt mystical, unexplainable, and disconnected from anything I saw around me.

During my undergraduate studies, however, I became deeply fascinated by cell biology. I spent an entire term immersed in an advanced course focused solely on the intricate workings of a single cell. *One* cell. The experience was awe-inspiring and opened my eyes to the profound complexity within us. Inside each cell, millions of orchestrated processes unfold on a microscopic scale, an entire world within.

It was then that I began to see the "magic dance" of energy that animates every living thing.

Every cell in our body is alive, intelligent, and constantly communicating. These trillions of cells form tissues, organs, and systems, all working in harmony (or disharmony) depending on the signals they receive.

Science tells us that cells respond not only to biochemical messages but also to energetic ones: vibration, frequency, and even thought. Our internal dialogue, the words we repeat to ourselves, directly impacts our physiology. When we're stressed, cells contract, energy tightens, and healing slows. When we feel safe and supported, cells relax and expand, creating space for growth and repair.

Even something as seemingly mundane as breathing reveals a complex web of energy exchange. Every inhale and exhale is part of an ongoing, invisible dance of life unfolding within us.

The miracle of cellular processes left me mesmerized.

As my studies deepened, I began to understand that everything we do, every action, thought, and interaction, is made up of energy. This isn't just a philosophical idea; it's a fundamental scientific truth. We are physical beings composed entirely of energy. And energy doesn't simply disappear; it transforms, shifts, and moves. But it is never destroyed.

The Potential of Energy

Looking closely at the structure of atoms reveals something astonishing: atoms, the building blocks of all life, are mostly empty space. If you were to expand an atom to the size of a football field, the nucleus would be a tiny dot at the center, while the electrons would be circulating somewhere around the bleachers. Everything in between? Empty space.

But it's not just any space, it's space filled with potential.

That void holds infinite possibilities. It's a powerful reminder that we, too, are filled with untapped potential. This isn't just a motivational phrase your parents told you; it's a truth grounded in science. And it's also… magical.

That same concept is what makes stem cell research so fascinating. Stem cells are considered "plastic," meaning they remain uncommitted until given a signal. Before a stem cell becomes a heart cell, a nerve cell, or a muscle cell, it exists as a blank slate, pure potential. The ability to shift and transform is where the magic happens: in the space between potential and directed outcome. This is energy transforming into form.

From Biology to Bio-Energy Healing

As I entered adulthood and pursued higher education, medicine seemed like the obvious path. It was a respectable, familiar route that fit neatly within society's expectations. I had wanted to make a positive impact towards bridging health gaps or improving health amongst humanity on a large scale, but deep down, biomedicine never fully aligned with the mystical visions I'd had as a child. Or the growing awareness I held about the deeper layers of healing beyond just the physical.

Without knowing what other paths were available to me, I studied furiously and took the MCAT twice. But something inside me started to stir. My intuition began pulling me in another direction. I couldn't ignore the overemphasis in modern healthcare on physical symptoms, the neglect of the whole person, and the widening gap between the values of the Hippocratic Oath and the reality I saw in the system.

There had to be another way to support people on their healing journeys, one that honored the whole being, including the energy systems often overlooked.

When Everything Shifted

My introduction to bio-energy healing came at a low point in my life, when anxiety and burnout had taken hold after I had followed a prescriptive path towards a career in medicine. While living in Vancouver in the midst of what I called my "mid-twenties crisis," I was questioning my life choices for the third time, overwhelmed by grief and loss, when I stumbled into my first energy healing session.

I met a woman named Victoria, a nurse by profession, who was also studying holistic health therapies. She lived across the street from me, and we had crossed paths several times through mutual friends. One day, she invited me to be a practice client for her bio-energy healing course. I was skeptical but agreed to be her guinea pig.

At the time, I didn't expect much. I was open to trying alternatives to allopathic medicine, but only mildly curious about what she was up to. I mainly wanted to support her in completing her program requirements.

What I didn't realize was that this session would change everything. It would open my eyes in a way I never anticipated and bring me full circle, back to the visions I'd had as a child.

A Powerful Awakening

Halfway through my first session, I experienced something I can only describe as a surge of energy, deep nausea, and an overwhelming sensation of tingling, warmth, and release. As Victoria continued her work, I found myself on the floor, kneeling, unable to stand, and confused. My entire body was vibrating, and I felt sick to my stomach.

The nausea lasted about five minutes before we could continue. In the pause between, I found myself in a state of disbelief. Did I eat something strange for lunch? What was happening in the pit of my stomach? There were two more moments during the session when I had to stop because of how intense these energy surges felt.

Throughout the remaining forty-five minutes, I kept wondering, "How could someone affect my body this way without even touching me?" Then, in a flash, I remembered the dream I had when I was five years old, healing someone with my hands.

I left that session feeling calm, yet still deeply confused. A few days later, I reached out to Victoria. But before she even had a chance to ask how I was doing, I blurted out, "Show me more."

When I Came to Trust Energy Healing

Though I had long sensed that health extended beyond the physical, my upbringing and education had trained me to think in conventional, material terms. I was used to treatments that targeted physical symptoms and body parts. So, the idea that energy could influence my health felt abstract.

But that session changed everything. I couldn't deny what I had experienced. Something real had happened, and intuitively, I knew there was more to explore.

Intrigued, I dove headfirst into the world of bio-energy healing, a practice that looks like a blend of Tai Chi and Reiki. I began learning about chakras, which are the body's energy centers that physically align with major organs and systems.

At first, I was skeptical. The word "chakra" had always felt a little "woo-woo" to me. But once I began to understand that these seven energy centers, running vertically from the base of the spine to the crown of the head, corresponded to dense areas of nerve plexuses and endocrine glands, it began to make perfect sense.

For example, the heart chakra isn't some mystical concept; it refers to the high concentration of energy surrounding the heart. As someone with a strong background in biology, this connection between science and spirituality finally clicked. What had once felt like separate worlds, energetics and anatomy, suddenly became beautifully integrated.

I began to realize that we don't have to rely solely on allopathic medicine. We have the power to influence our vitality from the inside out. Yes, we are that powerful.

The Body's Inherent Wisdom

This understanding deepened my belief in the profound intelligence of the body. I saw clearly that everything is interconnected: physical health, emotional stability, mental clarity, and spiritual alignment all operate within one vast energetic system.

Our bodies possess an innate drive toward healing and balance. But when we carry unresolved emotional wounds, mental stress, or spiritual disconnection, they can manifest as energetic blockages. Left unaddressed, these blockages often lead to physical pain, illness, or chronic dis-ease.

From Skepticism to Practice: Becoming a Bio-Energy Practitioner

As my curiosity grew, I couldn't get enough. I had finally found something that made sense on all levels, mind, body, and spirit. Before I knew it, I was enrolled in an energy healing practitioner program.

Working with people who were open to alternative methods, I saw how many were searching for something beyond pills and surface-level fixes. These clients wanted to understand and tap into the emotional and energetic layers influencing their well-being.

I resonated deeply with them. Like me, they were seeking to address the root causes of their health challenges, not just manage the symptoms. And that's what energy work offers: a path back to wholeness by starting from within.

By working with the body's energy field, we can help dissolve blockages and reawaken the body's natural healing potential. Again and again, I witnessed physical symptoms in people ease once energetic shifts occurred. Clients I worked with would leave sessions feeling lighter, more grounded, and often pain-free. These results only deepened my trust in the power of energy healing.

Honing Energy in the Body

A typical bio-energy healing session consists of four treatments. Over time, as I worked with clients, I learned to feel energy shifts in their bodies. Blocked areas would feel dense or sticky, and my hands would move more slowly when passing through these zones.

I learned to identify areas of imbalance or blockages in the body's major organs, which correspond to chakra centers. From there, the work of clearing and rebalancing energy would begin. The techniques used can vary: gentle hand movements, sweeping motions, subtle touch, or sometimes no touch at all, depending on the practitioner's style and the needs of the client.

When energy feels particularly dense or stagnant, I use my hands to "move" it, encouraging release and flow. With practice, I began to detect denser energy by the heat or even a kind of moisture that would accumulate around blocked areas.

Many clients would release tears during sessions as emotions and energy were cleared. This emotional release signals that energy is moving. Some clients also experienced vivid imagery, memories, or sensations. Ultimately, they would leave feeling lighter, relieved of pain, emotionally centered, or, in some cases, temporarily fatigued as their systems adjusted to the new energy balance.

The shifts were real and magical. Watching these transformations unfold deepened my fascination with energy and the potential we hold within.

Seeing the Whole Picture

As I continued to work with clients, I began noticing recurring patterns; how physical symptoms were very often intertwined with emotional states and belief systems.

For example, many of my clients with diabetes expressed feelings of bitterness, disillusionment, or a loss of "sweetness" in life. These emotions were often mirrored in how they spoke about themselves and their experiences. Some held deep-seated beliefs that life had no joy to offer or that they deserved to be punished. These internal belief systems create limitations in our minds, which in turn affect how our bodies respond.

Once I made these connections, everything began to make sense. Addressing emotional and belief-based patterns is just as important as addressing physical symptoms because all aspects of our system are connected. Remember, abracadabra means "with my word, I create." We can choose to think that life is without sweetness, or we can create a different version of our reality. It really does start from within. And we really are that powerful.

In another case, I worked with a client suffering from chronic hip pain. Despite trying every conventional method, her hip remained stiff and painful. During our sessions, we not only addressed her physical symptoms but also looked at what was happening in her life. She was resisting moving forward in her relationship and had internalized a fear of change. Her body was expressing this resistance through hip pain.

When we cleared the energy blockages surrounding that emotional resistance, her hip pain resolved. It was another powerful example of how emotions are just energy in motion and beliefs are deeply connected to physical health.

Let me be clear: I am not suggesting that people with diabetes or any medical condition should stop taking prescribed medications. What I am saying is that medication often addresses the physical manifestation but not the root cause. Energy work invites us to explore the full picture: physical, emotional, and spiritual.

If any of the stories I've shared have sparked curiosity about a physical ailment you haven't been able to resolve, I highly recommend exploring *The Body Talks* by Susan Aposhian and *You Can Heal Your Life* by Louise Hay. Both books offer a deeper understanding of the mind-body-spirit connection and highlight the importance of addressing all aspects of our being in the healing process.

Before I integrated coaching into my practice to help clients identify and reshape their belief systems, I worked in a clinic setting, offering people the chance to explore the mind-body-energy connection more deeply. One particularly memorable session involved a family physician experiencing burnout.

After five sessions, she began to connect the dots and recognized how blocked energy was contributing to her fatigue. Together, we worked to shift and release these energetic blockages, and she gradually regained a sense of vitality. She later shared this reflection:

"Prior to the sessions, I had a daily somatic practice for back pain and had taken a life-changing breathwork course, but something was still missing. After five sessions with Kassandra, I feel like all the pieces of the puzzle have come together.

I went on holiday with my family, and for the first time, I was able to truly relax and connect with them. I felt a physical freedom, like a straitjacket had been removed. Even after returning from the holiday, I continue to feel calmer, with a sense of physical freedom. When I breathe deeply, it feels bottomless and unconstricted. I'm now excited to explore energy and health more."

Dr. Layher

Feedback like this became powerful confirmation that energy work could profoundly affect not just physical symptoms, but mental and emotional health too. It also reaffirmed why I had been intuitively steered away from pursuing a career in Western medicine.

The Interconnectedness of All Things: Living and Healing From the Inside Out

Throughout my career as a bio-energy practitioner, I've seen the impact of energy work firsthand, from the subtle flow through my hands to the tangible shifts in a client's energy field. It felt like real magic.

I came to realize that physical symptoms often mirror deeper emotional or energetic imbalances, and true healing begins by observing our inner world (body, mind, and emotions) rather than focusing solely on our physical experience.

As my own journey evolved, I began to embody the inside-out approach to healing. I repeatedly witnessed how emotional and mental states manifest as physical symptoms, not just in my clients, but in myself. For example, my own anxiety often appears as tightness in my throat and a fluttering sensation in my heart. When I feel that constriction, I've learned to pause and listen.

I say to myself: *Thank you, body. I hear you.*

With this awareness, I use various tools that I'll share in upcoming chapters to return to a calmer, more grounded state. Over time, I've learned to recognize the intimate connection between my emotions, physical sensations, and mental patterns. Energy healing has helped me re-tune to a more peaceful version of myself.

Now, through a blend of energy healing and coaching, I guide clients to connect with their energetic systems, uncover root causes, and create sustainable change from the inside out.

Living from the inside out is how we reclaim our power to create lasting well-being.

Healing the Heart: Lessons from First Nations Communities

While working with First Nations communities, I was honored to witness traditional healing practices firsthand. I was invited to participate in a healing week, during which Indigenous and non-Indigenous practitioners came together to serve the community.

One of the most powerful experiences came during a session with a respected community chief. He had undergone multiple heart surgeries. When I assessed his energy, I noticed a heavy, stagnant presence around his heart. As we explored his emotional energy, it became clear that his physical condition was deeply connected to unresolved grief.

He shared that, as chief, he was responsible for facilitating funerals within his community, many of which were for young people lost to suicide. The weight of that grief was immense. His body was carrying the burden, and his heart was literally breaking under the pressure. He was on five different heart medications to treat his heart, but until the emotional aspect of grief was acknowledged, true healing of his heart was futile.

Indigenous cultures have long understood the interconnectedness of health. The medicine wheel, a traditional symbol, visually represents this holistic view. It reminds us that physical, mental, emotional, and spiritual well-being are inseparable. Unfortunately, Western medicine often isolates symptoms and overlooks this deeper, integrative understanding.

Bridging Science, Spirit, and Culture

I share these experiences because they represent the intersection of science, spirit, culture, and energy, and how all of these have shaped my perspective on healing from the inside out.

If this has sparked something within you, whether a new curiosity or a subtle shift in awareness, I encourage you to keep exploring. Stay open to the possibility that healing involves more than treating symptoms. It's about addressing the whole person.

It's been over a decade since my first bio-energy session, and my path in holistic healing continues to expand. My unique blend of energy work, belief system exploration, and coaching helps clients get to the root of physical illness and reconnect with their vitality.

By nurturing all aspects of ourselves, we tap into the power of our own energy. We begin transforming our lives at the source. From the inside out.

I've spoken about the importance of becoming aware of your own energy as the first of four phases in the inside-out journey. Let's now go deeper into what we may be holding in our bodies and why in the next chapter.

Chapter 5

Trauma & Body Cells:

You Can't Heal What You Don't Feel

"Trauma doesn't simply disappear. It lingers in the body,

passed down through generations like an invisible inheritance."

An Inherited Burden: Understanding Ancestral Trauma

For the first thirty years of my life, I struggled with anxiety and deep emotional challenges, often turning to therapy in an effort to unravel childhood memories and make sense of my inner world. I was aware that I held belief systems that no longer served me, such as the idea that if I controlled everything, I would be safe. I had experienced overwhelming anxiety and was desperate to understand it more deeply.

As part of the "understanding" phase of my inside-out healing journey, I became determined to uncover where these beliefs and feelings originated. I wanted to begin unraveling the internal patterns that held me back and find a more empowering way to live. Although I was already in therapy, I had a persistent gut feeling that there was still more to uncover. At times, it felt as though I had personally lived through the traumatic experiences my mother shared. Only later did I realize I was carrying the emotional weight of her past as my own.

To cope with the anxiety that stemmed from this vague but heavy emotional inheritance, feeling there was more beneath the surface, but not knowing what, I often turned to food for comfort, eating even when I wasn't hungry. As I got older, I began drinking excessively to soothe my overactive nervous system.

Shelley A. Kaehr, a leading author and lecturer on ancestral healing, notes that 50 percent of our personality is shaped by our DNA (Kaehr, 2020). Fifty percent. This simple yet powerful insight highlights the profound and invisible forces that shape not only who we are but also who we have the potential to become.

Over the past decade, my deepening understanding of ancestral healing has led me to a powerful realization: some of the trauma I carry isn't even mine. I believe many others share this experience unknowingly.

Had some of the pain I felt been passed down through generations, encoded in my very DNA? At the time, I lacked the language and awareness to frame this question. Recognizing this hidden legacy was essential in order to truly move forward free from the unconscious burden of inherited pain.

And yet, there is often little space in our culture to talk about how ancestral wounds impact future generations. Even less space exists to safely explore the shame and guilt that arise when we carry trauma we never directly experienced but nonetheless feel.

My personal inquiry began with questions about my own childhood, but soon evolved into a deeper exploration that required me to look further back.

The Cellular Memory of Trauma and Epigenetics

Trauma, whether it's experienced in overt or subtle forms, affects us on a cellular level. This is where the science of epigenetics becomes especially relevant.

The concept of intergenerational trauma — the idea that the pain of one person or family can be passed down through generations — helps explain why a child might react to stress or conflict in ways that mirror their parents' trauma responses. The body remembers, even when the conscious mind does not.

To illustrate this, I often turn to a metaphor from my background as a musician. Imagine our genes as a piano. The strings (our genetic code) are already in place. Epigenetic marks are like the keys being pressed: they determine which strings vibrate, which ones sing out, and which remain silent. These marks are shaped by life experiences, and remarkably, they can be passed down from one generation to the next (Mendelson & McEwen, 2020).

In the context of intergenerational trauma, this analogy takes on deep personal meaning. What does it mean to carry the weight of ancestral pain? How does it shape our lives, even when we have not directly lived through those events?

These questions are central to my story and to my journey of learning how to live from the inside out. Understanding the impact of inherited trauma has allowed me to begin releasing what was never mine to hold and to move forward with greater clarity, freedom, and peace.

Braving the Shadows: A Legacy of Trauma and Healing

Imagine growing up in a country where the painful truths of the past are buried, where history is selectively forgotten, and the real stories are only beginning to surface. I'm referring to the legacy of residential schools, a dark chapter in Canadian history, where the government, in partnership with various Christian religious organizations, developed and funded a system designed for the cultural assimilation of Indigenous people.

Churches were tasked with running these schools, often with minimal government oversight, granting them unchecked power over Indigenous children. These institutions were not simply schools; they were tools of forced assimilation. Their true purpose was to "civilize" Indigenous children by erasing their languages, cultures, and spiritual traditions.

At the core of this system was the aim to convert Indigenous children to Christianity. Church leaders believed Indigenous people needed to be saved, framing their traditional beliefs as inferior or even sinful. Catholic, Anglican, and other Christian denominations imposed their religion as the only truth while systematically denigrating Indigenous ways of life.

As extensively documented in the Truth and Reconciliation Commission (TRC, 2015), residential schools were sites of widespread physical, emotional, and sexual abuse. But the trauma didn't end when the doors to these schools closed. Instead, it seeped into families and communities, silently carried forward through generations. Like an invisible thread, this trauma wove itself into daily life, rippling outward in complex and painful ways.

In particular, Catholic-run schools have been at the center of numerous allegations of sexual abuse by priests and other religious staff. The authority of the Church made such crimes easy to hide; religious power was rarely questioned. In many cases, church officials were complicit in covering up physical and sexual abuse. The TRC revealed that many of the perpetrators were members of the clergy, and that religious authorities were often slow or unwilling to address these allegations. This silence only compounded the harm.

In my work within Indigenous health, I've come to more fully understand the profound and enduring legacy of Canada's residential school system. This was not merely a policy failure; it was cultural genocide. The intergenerational trauma it created continues to shape the lives of Indigenous families today. Acknowledging this pain is essential not just for the healing of individuals but for the collective healing of entire communities.

To put this in perspective, the last residential school in Canada closed in 1996. That is not distant history. The wounds left by these institutions are still raw, still affecting the children and grandchildren of survivors. Those who lived through the abuse often transmitted their trauma unconsciously, never fully understanding the shadows they were passing down.

In a culture steeped in colonial ignorance, harmful stereotypes such as "drunk Indian" or "natives mooching off the system" continue to erase historical context. These toxic labels obscure the root causes of behavior, ignoring the deep suffering that lies beneath. Such language doesn't just perpetuate ignorance; it inflicts further harm.

According to Indigenous teachings, it takes seven generations to heal intergenerational trauma (Duran, 2021). This aligns with the science of epigenetics, which shows that behaviors, belief systems, and trauma responses can be passed from one generation to the next.

Connecting the Dots: Family Ties

In my own family, the weight of history with the church is deeply felt. I recently learned that my great-grandfather on my mother's side was Chippewa. He attended a day school, one of many institutions designed to suppress Indigenous identity and subject children to cultural and physical abuse. From what my mother has shared, there was profound shame in our family around being even part Indigenous, driven by the societal prejudice that came with it.

I never met my grandfather on my mother's side — my great-grandfather's son — but I've heard stories about his childhood. He was a cute, curly-haired boy who once served as an altar boy at a church in London, Ontario. That same church, I later learned, was linked to known pedophile rings. Tragically, he became entangled in that cycle of abuse.

Whatever he endured within the church system, combined with the internalized shame about his Indigenous heritage, led him to make heartbreaking choices. He eventually married the "whitest" woman he could find, my Danish grandmother, in what seemed like an attempt to distance himself from the pain of his identity and escape societal prejudice. From what my mother has shared, my grandmother and grandfather were drawn together from familiar patterns of abuse in their families.

Trauma doesn't disappear just because we try to hide from it.

My grandfather carried his wounds forward and perpetuated abuse in his own family, physically and sexually harming his wife and daughters, including my mother. Eventually, she escaped the violence as a teenager. She lived on the streets for a time, working three jobs to put herself through school. She later earned a Ph.D. and wrote a book about her trauma.

I'm eternally proud of my mom's resilience. Growing up, she was my hero. She broke the cycle of physical and sexual abuse in the family, a cycle rooted in generational pain and buried history.

Fast forward to my upbringing. I grew up with privilege, there's no doubt about that. My mother, who was of Métis and Danish heritage, worked as an English professor. My father, a geologist, came from Scottish and Welsh roots. Although my parents divorced when I was young, I had everything I needed, and I'm genuinely grateful to them for that.

Growing up, though, I believed my life was pretty normal. That's why the unexplained emotional heaviness I carried felt so confusing. But now, with a deeper understanding of ancestral trauma, I can finally make sense of it.

Although I had access to opportunity and a certain level of comfort, I didn't fully grasp the emotional toll of the unresolved trauma my mother carried or how it impacted me until much later in life.

Connecting the Dots: My Personal Connection

The cycle of trauma in my family didn't continue through physical or sexual abuse, but it did manifest emotionally. I became my mother's anchor, absorbing her pain, trying to maintain peace at home, and feeling responsible for her well-being. I learned early on that I needed to protect not only myself but also her.

There were volatile moments when my mother would become upset over seemingly minor things. She could be warm and loving one moment, and then unexpectedly angry or hurtful the next, bringing up past grievances from months before. These outbursts felt unpredictable, and she often couldn't explain what was going on. As a child, I had to navigate this emotional chaos on my own. The message I internalized was that love could be taken away easily. It severely blurred my sense of boundaries.

I was often told that I "had it better" than she did, that I didn't have a reason to feel upset about anything in my childhood. This made me feel small and invalidated, and unsafe to be fully myself or allow myself to express what I was really feeling inside: the impact of a long line of family trauma.

I took on the role of peacekeeper, constantly trying to smooth things over to preserve a sense of stability. That pattern, coupled with my dad's lack of expressing love, led me to become a chronic people-pleaser.

I grew up fast. I normalized the emotional weight I was carrying, unaware that it wasn't mine to carry. It wasn't until my thirties that I realized pain is relative. Just because my trauma wasn't as visible or extreme as my mother's didn't mean it wasn't real. I may not have experienced the same abuse, but the emotional burden I bore was still significant.

In my early years, I developed coping mechanisms like emotional eating. Later, alcohol became a way to soothe my overactive nervous system. I didn't yet understand that the discomfort in my body wasn't solely caused by my present-day stress. Yes, the pressure of modern life, especially the relentless pace of technology and social media, added to my overwhelm. But the root of it ran deeper.

Over the past few years, as I explored ancestral healing, I began to see that the true work of healing lies in confronting the wounds that didn't start with me. I realized I was carrying the unresolved pain of those who came before me, encoded in my very DNA. For a long time, I had overlooked the fact that I carried cells from my mother's womb. Those cells remembered. This realization was both profound and validating.

Breaking the Cycle and Reclaiming Our Inner Power

A major turning point in my healing came when I understood that true healing isn't just about the mind; it must include being present in the body. In a society that teaches us to suppress emotions and intellectualize pain, we often forget the body's wisdom. The body constantly speaks to us through tension, illness, discomfort, and emotional signals. Healing requires more than eating well or exercising; it requires tuning into the body's messages.

I've learned to nourish my emotional well-being through daily practices like self-reflection, meditation, and bodywork techniques. These practices have helped me connect to the pain stored in my body and, in doing so, begin the process of releasing it.

The final piece of the puzzle fell into place during what I've come to call the "understanding" phase of the Inside Out approach. Once I truly grasped the deeper roots of my behaviors, emotions, and coping patterns, I was ready to step into the third phase: breaking free.

In the following chapters, I'll share tools and strategies that can help you identify and express your emotions. Through cultivating self-awareness and facing our emotional wounds, we can begin to break the cycles of generational pain. We can live from the inside out with authenticity, clarity, autonomy, and freedom.

Once we understand the deeper layers of ourselves, we can finally choose to reclaim our power and align our lives with what we truly desire. We can start to create magic in our lives, from the inside out.

Part 3

Breaking Free

Chapter 6

Finding Freedom in the Space between:

Reclaiming Your Response

"Our choice resides in the crucial space between stimulus and reaction."

Let's pause for a moment before diving into the third phase of the Inside Out approach, breaking free, and reflect on what we've explored so far.

In today's turbulent world, external events like political unrest, social instability, and global crises are increasingly shaping our mental health. These pressures, amplified by political polarization and the rise of social media, can fuel heightened anxiety and a deep sense of powerlessness (Keltner et al., 2019).

Paradoxically, as we become more digitally connected, many of us feel increasingly isolated. Online spaces often encourage carefully curated, idealized versions of ourselves, replacing vulnerability with polished images. Despite our growing reliance on digital tools to stay "connected," they can exacerbate mental health challenges. Algorithms designed to capture our attention often trigger emotional responses, intensifying anxiety, reinforcing echo chambers, and distorting our perception of reality. In such an environment, confusion and emotional disconnection are not only common, they're almost inevitable.

But the effects go deeper than just emotional well-being. The digital world and broader external chaos affect our entire being, including our physical health.

When our nervous systems are overwhelmed by external stressors, it's natural to respond from a place of fear. We've discussed how, in response to fear, many of us seek control. Ironically, these control mechanisms often stem from the very anxiety we're trying to escape. Whether the stress comes from politics, technology, interpersonal conflict, or global instability, it's essential to recognize the interconnectedness of our physical, emotional, mental, and spiritual health. These elements are not separate; they influence each other continuously. The energy of our inner world even has the power to impact illness. And often, these forces are shaped by inherited or invisible traumas that we carry without even realizing it.

So, how do we navigate this complexity and reclaim our agency?

We have a choice: to confront discomfort and explore how external forces shape our internal world, or to remain passive, swept up in the current. This choice marks the beginning of the path to breaking free.

With the nonstop bombardment of technology and social media, it can be hard to see clearly through the fog. It takes courage to step out of reaction mode and into conscious awareness.

Transforming from the Inside Out

As we begin peeling back the layers of our lived experience, we must ask: How can we thrive in a world where authenticity seems to be fading? What happens to our mental health when vulnerability is replaced by filters and curated lives?

To begin transforming, we must learn to pause to slow our reactions, reflect, and shift from autopilot to intention. This is how we start breaking away from the default responses and begin choosing how we want to live.

Self-reflection, awareness, and understanding form the first step toward transformation. They allow us to begin intentionally creating, acting, and living from the inside out, rather than reacting to whatever the external world throws our way.

While the external world certainly shapes our experiences, it's our inner world, our beliefs, thought patterns, and emotional habits that ultimately determine our response. And that's where our power lies.

We do have the ability to choose how we respond to life's challenges. Between stimulus and response, there is a brief but powerful pause, a space of potential. In that pause, we can choose whether to act out of fear or intention.

This pause is not passive. It is an active choice to shift from automatic reaction to conscious awareness. This ability to pause and choose is the turning point between living in reaction mode and living from the inside out.

Whether it's taking a breath before responding to a triggering comment or stopping to reflect during a moment of overwhelm, the pause creates space for intentional action. In this way, it helps break the cycle of fear-driven reactivity and allows us to respond from a grounded, calm place.

The pause is also supported by research. Mindfulness and cognitive-behavioral practices like Mindfulness-Based Stress Reduction (MBSR) have shown that when we learn to pause and observe our emotional responses without acting on them right away, we reduce anxiety and improve emotional regulation (Kabat-Zinn, 2003).

Neuroscience reinforces this idea. Engaging the prefrontal cortex, the part of the brain responsible for decision-making and impulse control during mindfulness practices, helps us override automatic, fear-based responses (Zeidan et al., 2010).

The pause is vital because when we feel empowered to choose our actions and decisions, we are far less likely to succumb to helplessness or chronic anxiety. Each time we consciously respond rather than react, we reclaim our agency and begin to break down overwhelming challenges into manageable steps.

When we experience heightened emotional reactions, especially during tense situations or conflicts, it's often not just the present moment influencing us. For example, during an argument, rather than reacting defensively, we can pause to assess our emotional state: Are we feeling unheard? Are old wounds being triggered?

Unresolved trauma, past hurts, and emotional scars can be activated by current events, even when those events seem unrelated. These emotional triggers can make our reactions feel disproportionate or irrational because they're tied to deeper, often subconscious, memories and experiences.

By taking a moment to pause, we create the space to respond with empathy, de-escalate tension, and foster understanding. This is the essence of the second phase of the Inside Out approach, breaking free, and it's a pivotal, empowering step towards living from a place of alignment and inner power. So, how do we do this?

A Tool for Investigation: Reclaiming Our Power

One invaluable tool I use regularly in the practice of pausing is the RAIN technique, a simple yet powerful method for recognizing and responding to difficult emotions:

- **Recognize** the emotion
- **Accept** its presence
- **Investigate** its origins
- **Nurture** self-compassion

Introduced by psychologist and meditation teacher Tara Brach, RAIN has become a cornerstone of my emotional wellness practice (Brach, 2020). When external events trigger anxiety or emotional unrest, RAIN offers a clear structure to pause, acknowledge what's arising, and move forward with compassion. Research shows that self-compassion can significantly reduce emotional distress and improve psychological well-being.

Let's walk through an example.

A Scenario: Using RAIN in Real Life

Imagine you've just had a heated conversation with a friend, and you're feeling unsettled afterward. Here's how you might apply RAIN:

1. **Recognize**

    You notice a racing heart and discomfort. You acknowledge: "This is anxiety."

2. **Accept**

    Instead of resisting the feeling, you allow it. "It's okay to feel this way. I'm human."

3. **Investigate**

    You gently explore: "Am I afraid of being misunderstood? Of losing the relationship? Is a past conflict being triggered? What's the story I'm telling myself right now?"

4. **Nurture**

    You offer kindness to yourself. "It's okay to feel anxious. I'm doing my best, and I get to choose how to respond."

By practicing RAIN, we interrupt the cycle of reactivity and create space for grounded, compassionate responses. This process doesn't have to take a long time. Often, I notice the urge to react and take just a few moments to check in with my body. I may even ask for a few minutes away from the conversation to process what I'm feeling. With practice, this becomes easier, and you'll begin identifying what's happening inside you more quickly.

After moving through the RAIN steps, I'm far more able to express myself clearly rather than reacting from a flood of emotion.

Practicing RAIN with Everyday Triggers

I also apply RAIN in moments of heightened anxiety, such as when reading a distressing news article. Instead of continuing to scroll and letting fear compound, I pause:

- I recognize the fear arising (R).
- Accept that it's okay to feel unsettled (A).
- Investigate where the fear is coming from, perhaps childhood memories or fear of uncertainty (I).
- And nurture myself by offering reassurance: "I'm safe right now. It's okay to feel scared." (N)

This practice is powerful, especially in today's fast-paced world, where emotional triggers are everywhere.

Consider making RAIN part of your daily life:

- Before checking your phone in the morning, take a minute to practice RAIN with any anxiety about the day ahead.
- When you're feeling social anxiety in public, excuse yourself to the restroom and take a moment to check in.
- During conversations when stress rises, use RAIN to ground yourself before you respond.

In Summary

Though our default may be to react impulsively, we always have the power to pause, observe our thoughts, and consciously choose how we respond. That space between stimulus and response is where our freedom begins to take shape.

When you start to use this practice on a regular basis, it is a sign that you are entering the third phase of the Inside Out journey: breaking free. This is where the magic begins. It is the point at which you choose to start living from the inside out. It's the breakthrough moment.

Because your **power** is in the **pause**.

As we work with the fears and anxieties triggered by external events, we must also confront the subconscious stories that shape how we respond. In the next chapter, we'll explore the hidden patterns and internal narratives that influence our reactions and how we can begin rewriting them to transform how we operate and navigate the world around us.

Chapter 7

Breaking Free from the Scripts:
Patterns & Conditions

"By recognizing these deeply ingrained patterns, we can begin to break free from their limiting influence and embrace a more authentic and fulfilling life."

Recognizing Inherited Patterns

Our behaviors are often shaped by the stories we inherit from societal norms, cultural beliefs, and family teachings. These invisible scripts influence how we perceive and interact with the world, often without our conscious awareness. While these patterns may have once served a purpose, they may no longer be in our best interest. Recognizing this is a critical part of the *breaking free* phase of living from the inside out. It's how we begin to transform our behaviors and move toward the life we truly want to live.

Let's look at subconscious patterns rooted in early childhood experiences or formative relationships. For example, if your parents were emotionally distant or critical, you may have internalized the painful belief that you are unworthy of love or care. As adults, these internalized beliefs can subtly and sometimes significantly shape how we relate to others and how we react under stress.

Uncovering the Narratives

One way to recognize these subconscious patterns is to explore the narratives you hold about yourself, especially those rooted in feelings of inadequacy, fear of failure, or perfectionism. Journaling, therapy, and inner child work are powerful tools for uncovering and rewriting these deeply ingrained stories. As I encourage my clients to do in my "Burnout to Breakthrough" group program, observe yourself over a week to recognize moments when you are reactive, triggered, or overwhelmed. Take notes in a journal over the week to start capturing data. Once you have done this, start to see if there are patterns or themes which emerge.

As we begin to recognize the beliefs, behaviors, and expectations passed down through generations, this awareness becomes a catalyst for growth. It gives us the opportunity to get curious and question the assumptions we've inherited so we can consciously choose patterns that align with our current values and aspirations.

For instance, one of the most deeply ingrained subconscious patterns I absorbed in childhood was the need to prioritize safety. This came from both of my parents: from my father, it was financial safety, a belief shaped by his own parents, who lived through war. From my mother, it was the need for emotional safety and self-protection, especially in relation to others. Her trauma taught me, subconsciously, to protect myself in relationships, to never allow true vulnerability.

These kinds of patterns were once useful. They helped us survive. But as we evolve, many of them no longer serve us. In fact, they can actively hold us back. For example, if you grew up in an environment where love felt conditional, you may find yourself subconsciously fearing rejection even in safe, loving adult relationships. Without realizing it, you may gravitate toward partners who mirror that conditional love, perpetuating the same painful cycle.

When stated plainly, it may seem irrational. But this is how the brain works. Neural pathways formed through early experiences become default operating systems. Unless we consciously update them, we continue to run on outdated programming.

Rewriting the Story

When we commit to curiosity and self-reflection, we begin to unravel these outdated patterns and make space to write new stories. This shift allows us to move beyond performing in the "doing" of roles or meeting expectations and step into a deeper sense of *being*. We are, after all, human beings - not human doings.

To live authentically, we must shed the limitations of inherited beliefs and forge our own path. A great place to begin is with daily reflection. By observing your recurring behaviors, thoughts, and emotional triggers, you can begin to see which patterns are no longer aligned with who you are or who you want to become.

The How: Tools and Techniques

Below are some tools and strategies I've personally used and continue to use to get where I am today. I hope they inspire you to explore the deeper parts of yourself that may be standing in the way of living in alignment with your true desires.

Journaling Prompts

Use these questions to begin unpacking subconscious beliefs:

- "What beliefs or behaviors am I holding onto about worth, my voice, or success that no longer serve me? What am I afraid to let go of, and why?"

- "Which beliefs empower me? Which ones limit my growth?"

- Where did this belief begin? What is the origin of this story?

This type of introspection can be a powerful catalyst for transformation. As you start to plainly see that you are defaulting to running on an old operating system, you will begin to understand that your inner software needs an update. The old software is outdated. This type of realization is an important step towards aligning your actions with your values, and supports a more authentic, fulfilling life.

Write Down Behaviors

Next, identify the coping behaviors you developed to survive emotionally difficult situations growing up. These might include:

- People-pleasing

- Perfectionism

- Avoiding conflict

- Overachieving

- Shutting down emotionally

Once you identify them, you can begin to assess whether they're still serving you or keeping you stuck. Perhaps there is a better way for you to get what you want. You can look at the deeper need underneath the behavior and ask questions like, "What need am I trying to meet in acting out in this way?" Get curious, and keep asking why.

Therapy or Coaching

Work with a therapist or coach (such as myself) who is experienced in identifying and helping shift or rewire subconscious patterns. Some survival mechanisms are so deeply embedded that they're hard to detect on your own. We all have blind spots. That's why having a supportive and reflective community is invaluable. It helps you uncover blind spots you can't see because you're living inside them.

Community

Set an intention to break free from old automatic reactions, and share that intention with someone you trust, a coach, therapist, or close friend. Ask them to help hold you accountable. Together, you can create a list of healthier, more conscious responses you'd like to adopt. Check in regularly to reflect on your progress and adjust your approach as needed.

Create Empowering Affirmations

Once you've uncovered limiting beliefs (e.g., "I'm unworthy of love"), write positive affirmations to counter them. For example, replace that belief with: "I am worthy and deserve to receive love." Repeat this affirmation daily. Say it out loud, write it in your journal, or post it somewhere visible. Over time, you will train your subconscious mind to absorb and internalize this new, empowering narrative. I do this all the time.

Gradual Exposure

As you identify healthier response patterns, start practicing them in low-stakes situations. If you have a history of avoiding confrontation due to childhood conditioning, begin by asserting yourself in small ways. Practice voicing your needs or respectfully disagreeing with someone. These small steps will build confidence and retrain your nervous system to tolerate vulnerability and assertiveness.

Inner Child Work

The inner child represents the part of you that still holds unmet needs from childhood. It's the emotional imprint of your younger self, still longing for validation, comfort, and safety. Set aside quiet time once a week to connect with this part of yourself. Close your eyes and visualize yourself as a child. Ask: *What did I need that I didn't receive?* Speak to your younger self with kindness and compassion. Offer them the words and support they needed to hear then and still need now.

Personally, people-pleasing is a coping behavior for getting love and acceptance. I spoke earlier as to why this may be the case (family modeling behaviors), but now I recognize that a healthier behavior is to give myself love and acceptance so that I don't need to get it externally in a potentially destructive way.

In my coaching practice, I've seen that one of the deepest wounds women carry is the fear of taking up too much space or being "too much." For men, the core wound often centers on feeling like they're never "enough." These beliefs are deeply influenced by cultural norms and societal expectations, but we don't have to inherit them blindly.

By examining how early experiences and cultural conditioning shaped your sense of self-worth, emotions, and behaviors, you can begin to understand and release the subconscious drivers of your reactions.

Rewriting the Script

It's fascinating how far back our core stories go. But by understanding their origins, we can begin to free ourselves from their grip. Awareness gives us the power to begin to choose differently so we can align with the life we truly want to live, from the inside out.

It requires courage, patience, and a willingness to challenge long-held assumptions. But the rewards are immense.

The Power of Self-Reflection

Breaking free from ingrained habits can be uncomfortable at first. It may even feel like you're risking love or acceptance, especially if people around you react negatively to your changes. But remember: if they are true allies, they will support your growth. And if they don't? That wasn't real love to begin with.

If you're ready to go deeper, make self-reflection a daily practice. Over time, it becomes a natural part of how you relate to yourself and the world around you. Here's how:

Self-Awareness Practices

1. **Morning Intention Setting**

   Start your day by setting a clear intention to observe your reactions and behaviors, particularly in triggering situations. This proactive step enhances self-awareness and helps you respond more mindfully.

2. **Evening Reflection**

   Spend 10 minutes at the end of your day reviewing your experiences. Ask yourself:

   - What behaviors or reactions did I notice today that may have been influenced by past experiences or family conditioning?
   - Did I act in alignment with the person I want to become?
   - If not, what pattern do I need to shift?

Mindful Observation (Weekly Practice)

Continue to track moments during the week where you noticed yourself acting out of habit, avoiding conflict, overcompensating, shutting down, etc. Pay attention to the emotional charge in those moments. Use the RAIN technique to process what arises: Recognize, Accept, Investigate, and Nurture.

For me, this entire process felt clunky at first. I struggled to prioritize time with myself in the mornings. I had convinced myself that I simply didn't have the time. But when someone pointed out that people make time for what they prioritize, I had to get honest: I wasn't prioritizing myself. That realization was pivotal. Once I committed to changing my behavior and truly prioritized my growth, real progress followed.

The more you observe your patterns and reflect on your actions, the clearer things will become. With this awareness, you'll be empowered to make conscious choices about how you want to operate in the world.

And my guess? You'll probably want to adjust a few things.

Breaking Free from Childhood Conditioning

When I did these exercises, I realized I had received a message early on that I was "too much." In response, I learned to suppress my natural exuberance in order to gain acceptance. This created a lifelong pattern of "playing small" to avoid disapproval.

I prioritized others' needs and approval, which was behavior I carried into adulthood without even realizing it. This people-pleasing persona, while originally a survival mechanism, ultimately prevented me from living authentically.

Putting other people first came at a cost. Over time, I lost touch with my own needs and desires. It wasn't until much later that I recognized I had built emotional walls around my true self, trying to shield that part of me from rejection. While this coping strategy once served me, it gradually became a barrier to growth. Realizations like these allow us to better understand ourselves and invite us to question whether it's time to shift how we operate in the world.

As a musician and singer, I've also struggled with the subconscious belief that my voice wasn't worthy of being heard. I feared judgment not just from others, but from myself. This pattern traces back to childhood experiences that taught me to stay small to avoid criticism. The women in my family lineage also weren't comfortable speaking out, which is an all-too-common story.

Maybe you've felt similarly, avoiding the spotlight, holding back your voice, or hiding your full self. My mother still sometimes comments that I must love being in the spotlight. The truth is, it takes conscious effort every single time I step on stage. And that's exactly why I continue to sing. It's not because it comes naturally, but because performing is a part of my healing process. Singing allows me to break through old patterns of feeling unsafe in expressing myself or being seen. It's how I reclaim my power and choose to move beyond inherited narratives.

Another pattern I've carried since childhood stems from my relationship with my father, who was emotionally unavailable. This created a core belief that I was always waiting for the men in my life to truly show up for me. Unsurprisingly, it impacted my relationships. I often found myself drawn to emotionally distant partners. The truth is, we are more likely to attract what feels familiar rather than what we truly desire. That's the power of these childhood patterns and our trained neuropathways.

I share these reflections as examples of the kinds of insights that can surface when you engage with the journaling prompts and daily practices I shared earlier. These exercises are not just about self-awareness, they're about liberation.

The good news? These survival mechanisms don't have to define us. With awareness, intention, and courage, we can challenge and gradually release them. That's where the journey of breaking free begins.

How Life Can Look After

Today, I have a morning practice. Each day, I spend time journaling, reflecting, tuning in, and deciding how I want the day to unfold. I put myself in the driver's seat and suddenly, I have all the time and presence in the world.

Tools like affirmations, journaling, talk therapy, breathing exercises, and mindfulness have helped me uncover and reprogram subconscious beliefs in a way that feels manageable and empowering. These practices don't just help you understand yourself better, they help you come home to yourself.

So, what's on the other side of all this courage and hard work?

You will feel in charge of your life again. You'll show up for yourself and for your loved ones in a more authentic and empowered way. You'll stop operating from the past and start intentionally creating a life you're excited to live. I know for myself, when I was asking myself "what is all this for?" and "what do I really want," I was yearning for connection…with myself. From that place, I can truly live a life that feels aligned. And when my own cup is full and my inner world is balanced, I can start to look outside myself. I can work on contributing an aligned version of myself to the world and start creating positive ripple effects from the inside out.

Yes, it's possible. I've done it. I come back to these practices when I fall off track, and I support others in doing the same.

But first, we must break free from our internal limitations. We must "unstuck" ourselves before we can fully access the peace, freedom, and joy we long for.

I invite you to embrace this journey with patience and compassion. Start small. Celebrate progress. And always, always practice self-compassion. It takes tremendous courage to live from the inside out, but if you've made it this far, you're already deep into the *breaking free* phase.

You are well on your way.

Now, let's explore some real-life examples of how patterns show up in our lives and how to recognize and reshape them so they align with your truest, most authentic self. Living from the inside means recognizing and rewriting inherited scripts, a powerful step toward lasting fulfillment.

Chapter 8

Breaking Free from the Scripts:
The Good Girl and Sabotage Patterns

"The journey of self-discovery and untangling outdated patterns is about progress, not perfection."

The "Good Girl" Script: A Legacy of Limiting Beliefs

Now that we have explored subconscious patterning and examined our own behaviors from childhood, I want to share a bit about my own conditioning and how I came to understand the roots of my people-pleasing tendencies. I'll begin with my paternal grandmother.

Inheriting the Role of the Good Girl

My grandmother (on my dad's side) and I shared a deep love and respect for one another. However, our lives were shaped by different eras and perspectives. She married young, raised two sons, and devoted herself to domestic life. In contrast, I pursued higher education and an independent path, seeking opportunities she never had.

My grandmother, Violet, was a woman of immense strength and resilience, yet she was deeply influenced by the societal expectations of her time. These expectations pushed her to dedicate her life to caregiving, often, I believe, at the expense of her own dreams and desires.

She frequently expressed how proud she was of my achievements in university, sports, and my career. But I could sense, in her eyes, a longing for the opportunities she had to forego. I believe she possessed a deep well of untapped potential and a creative spirit yearning to be explored.

I, on the other hand, was raised by a feminist mother who encouraged my independence and academic pursuits. Because my grandmother and I lived such different lives, our interactions didn't always resonate. When I was younger, I didn't think we had much in common. Yet despite our differing circumstances, a subtle yet powerful force shaped both our lives: the pressure to conform, to play within limits, and to keep ourselves small.

Living the Role

I, too, fell prey to the "good girl" script seeking validation from strict parents with high expectations, teachers who saw potential in me, and a society that promoted the message: do more, buy more, and achieve more.

In striving for perfection, chasing grades, conforming to expectations, and pleasing everyone around me, I unknowingly adopted the "good girl" persona, believing it was the key to acceptance and love.

Cracks in the Role

While it appeared harmless, embodying the good girl persona quietly stifled the real me. This deeply ingrained pattern, passed down through generations, can have profound and lasting impacts, and I have experienced this firsthand.

Patterns reveal how deeply connected we are to our upbringing and lived experiences. I want to take this reflection a step further.

As mentioned, my grandmother's life, while filled with love and dedication, may have been constrained by societal expectations and the limitations of her time. Later in life, she was diagnosed with Parkinson's disease, a degenerative condition marked by worsening tremors.

At the time, I didn't fully grasp the impact of her illness. But as I deepened my study into the interconnectedness of our physical, emotional, and spiritual health, I came across the work of Louise Hay.

Hay's holistic approach in *You Can Heal Your Life* suggests that unexpressed anger and frustration may contribute to physical ailments like Parkinson's disease. This was a lightbulb moment for me. Could my grandmother's suppressed desires and unfulfilled potential have contributed to or somehow connected with her physical condition?

Breaking the Cycle

As I reflected on this possibility, a crucial question arose: Why do we limit ourselves to lives that don't fully honor our true selves? Why do we hide who we are and conform to others' expectations?

The answer is complex. Historically, it hasn't always been safe, especially for women, to speak out, express anger, or break free from social and familial norms.

I know I'm not alone in feeling the subconscious restraints of holding back my true and powerful self. But once we become aware of these patterns, we have a choice: remain trapped in them or shift the narrative and break free.

My grandmother may be gone, but her spirit continues to guide me. In my meditations, I often connect with her, honoring the strength and resilience she embodied despite the limitations she faced.

Inspired by her life and my own journey of self-discovery, I am committed to breaking free from these inherited constraints. I strive to live authentically, embrace my true self, and empower others to do the same.

Let me tell you, though it's not easy. It takes practice.

Rewriting the Role – Tools and Techniques

If you're on your own journey of self-discovery, I invite you to examine the family scripts or inherited beliefs that have shaped your life. What patterns no longer serve you? Which ones will you rewrite to reflect your authentic self?

The power is in your hands.

Suggestions for Diving Deeper

- **Family Interview**: If possible, talk to family members (parents, grandparents, etc.) about their experiences and beliefs. Listen for patterns in how they talk about love, money, success, or self-worth. This can offer valuable insight into inherited values or limitations.

- **Rewrite Your Family Script**: Once you've identified limiting family patterns, write a new script for yourself. For instance, if your family believed that "only hard work equals success," you might rewrite it as: Success is a combination of hard work, creativity, and rest.

Read this new script aloud daily to begin internalizing it.

Take time to reflect on your family history. How have the experiences and beliefs of your ancestors shaped your worldview? What patterns have been passed down through generations? In what ways have you forced yourself to fit in?

You'll likely encounter resistance during this process. These ingrained patterns, deeply rooted in our subconscious, have been shaping our behavior for years. It takes conscious effort to break free from them. Be patient with yourself. It won't happen overnight.

As you begin to recognize the limits of any inherited identity, you may notice how you unconsciously create obstacles to your own happiness. In an effort to feel protected (because change can be scary), we sometimes sabotage our own success.

Identifying Self-Sabotage Patterns

Have you ever set a goal, only to find yourself undermining your own efforts? Maybe you talk yourself out of pursuing your dreams, or you prioritize others' needs at the expense of your own. This is known as self-sabotage.

Through my work with clients, I've identified three recurring self-sabotaging patterns that many of us unconsciously engage in:

- **The Martyr Syndrome**: This pattern causes us to prioritize others' needs over our own, often leading to burnout, resentment, and a deep sense of being unappreciated. It's a subtle form of self-sabotage, where you unknowingly sacrifice your goals to avoid conflict or maintain an image of selflessness.

- **The Reward-Punishment Cycle**: This shows up in extremes, you push yourself relentlessly, only to "reward" yourself with excessive indulgence, effectively negating your progress. This back-and-forth between self-discipline and self-destruction can feel like an endless loop.

- **The People-Pleasing Trap**: Driven by a fear of losing love or approval, this pattern makes it incredibly difficult to say "no." You end up compromising your own values and desires just to maintain social harmony. This was a significant struggle for me, rooted in childhood experiences where being "good" and playing small were strongly rewarded.

Why Do We Engage in Self-Sabotaging Behaviors?

A major factor is social conditioning. From a young age, we learn which behaviors are rewarded and which are punished. Over time, these lessons solidify into deeply ingrained patterns that unconsciously shape our choices.

For me, people-pleasing began in childhood as a response to a mother who had endured significant trauma and a father who was physically absent, emotionally unavailable, and not great with children.

If I acted as a source of emotional support for my mother, displaying patience, wisdom, and care, I was rewarded with love and affection. But if I triggered her trauma, she would become extremely reactive, sometimes storming out or cutting off contact for hours or even weeks.

My father worked away from home, and when he was around, I was desperate for his attention. I would proudly show him my school grades, hoping for a sign of approval that I was a "good girl." I remember one moment vividly: I had earned an "A" on a test and eagerly showed it to him. He glanced at it and said, "Next time, you can aim for an A+."

That response crushed me. I felt like I wasn't good enough, as if something was wrong with me. And unfortunately, that wasn't an isolated incident. It became a pattern. Whenever I said, "I love you, Dad," his response was "Tough." It still is actually, now that I think about it.

The story I told myself was that if I acted like an adult around my dad and did everything perfectly, maybe one day I would earn his approval. He was emotionally detached and poor at communicating, so I was constantly trying to engage him, asking questions, seeking connection, but I was often met with disapproval or silence.

I want to emphasize that I don't hold any hard feelings toward my parents. I know they were both doing the best they could with the life experiences and patterns they inherited. That said, I now understand why I developed such strong people-pleasing tendencies.

I have a lot of love for both of my parents. Today, I accept them for who they are, and I don't blame them for anything. Holding onto blame only prolonged my own suffering. However, acknowledging the root causes of some of my behaviors requires honesty about the environment I grew up in, especially because, by my late twenties, the pain of constant people-pleasing had become unbearable. I often felt drained, resentful, and out of alignment with my true self.

That realization was a turning point.

Letting go of the good girl wasn't a loss, it was enchantment. A return to the wild, wise woman I had always been.

Rebuilding Relationships

Today, I have a great relationship with my dad partly because he's better with adults, but also because I stopped seeking his approval and started living my own life. When I created space to reframe how I viewed our relationship, I began to recognize his strengths and the ways he supported me in his own way.

Ironically, I think he respects me more now for being my own person, for being decisively me, even though we're quite different. And oddly the same in some respects. Funny thing about genetics.

I'd be lying if I said I've had the same success with my mom in terms of breaking free from people-pleasing and certain toxic cycles. But we love each other very much, and progress is happening. We've had some powerful breakthrough moments in both of our healing journeys this past year, and that gives me a lot of hope.

How to Break Free from Self-Sabotage

Breaking free from self-sabotaging patterns requires conscious effort and self-awareness. It's about recognizing your triggers, developing healthier coping mechanisms, and learning to honor your own needs and desires. With time, you can develop strategies to notice when you're self-sabotaging and redirect those behaviors into self-empowering actions.

Here are a few suggestions:

- **Self-Sabotage Tracking**:

  In your journal, track your actions and decisions, especially moments where you may have sabotaged your progress (e.g., procrastinating, overworking, avoiding boundaries). Pay attention to any underlying fears or limiting beliefs.

- **Redirection Practice**:

  Once you identify a pattern, create an action plan. For example, if you procrastinate when success feels close, break tasks into smaller steps and celebrate each small win to build momentum.

- **Accountability Partner**:

  Find a trusted friend, mentor, or coach to check in with regularly about your goals. External support can help counteract self-sabotaging tendencies like people-pleasing or conflict avoidance.

It's not just about deciding to be introspective. It takes intentional effort to rewire your brain and shift subconscious patterns that may have been running your life for years, so stick with it. You won't have it all figured out right away, and that's okay. You'll learn how to manage these behaviors and fine-tune your approach over time, but some patterns may not disappear completely.

Because the journey of self-discovery and unlearning outdated cycles and patterns is about progress, not perfection. As my bio-energy teacher once said, *"Practice makes permanent, not perfect."*

Also, everything I'm sharing with you are things that I continually need to come back to and practice. I have a quote hanging on my mirror that says, *"Rome wasn't built in a day, but they worked on it every day."* That's the reminder I return to often.

The point is to free yourself more and more each day from old neural pathways that no longer serve you so that you can create the vision and life that you want and deserve. While this process can bring up discomfort, impatience, frustration, and even pain, the outcome is worth it.

Letting go of the "good girl" doesn't mean losing who you are. It means finding your true voice, expressing it freely, and taking up space in a new, powerful way. Because the person who emerges after shedding the good girl role is strong, confident, and grounded. She moves through life with ease, creates a life that feels authentic, and inspires others to do the same.

You'll discover new passions, a renewed sense of purpose, and fresh ways to fulfill your potential as the incredible person you already are.

It's time to stop hiding.

Now that we've explored how subconscious patterns and behaviors can limit authentic living, let's shift our focus to a crucial next step in this work: understanding the concept of *payoffs*.

What exactly are payoffs, and why is it essential to identify yours?

Chapter 9

Breaking Free from the Payoff of Stagnation:
Embracing Change and Growth

"Two things can (and do) co-exist. Yes, I was excited, but I was also scared. This is the duality, the yin and yang, the balance."

The Story of "Not Enough"

From an early age, many of us internalize the belief that we are not enough; conditioned by family, society, and culture, we learn to seek approval, perfection, and validation as if they were prerequisites for worthiness. Over time, this belief becomes an identity, a story we carry with us. Not because it serves us, but because it feels familiar.

This story can be difficult to detect. You might, for instance, carry resentment toward a parent, convinced they didn't love you enough. That anger, while painful, gives you something: a story, a purpose, a form of self-definition. In a strange way, it can feel safer to hold onto pain than to face the vulnerability beneath it.

Pause here.

What story are you still carrying?

Even when we consciously want to change, our subconscious minds often resist. These protective inner voices stir up fear, anxiety, and discomfort, not because they're cruel, but because they believe they're keeping us safe. Change doesn't begin with action. It begins with the willingness to examine the beliefs and the emotional payoffs standing in the way.

The Hidden Force Behind Staying Stuck: Payoffs

We've already explored patterns like "playing the good girl" and "self-sabotage." But there's another hidden force that often keeps us stuck: the payoff.

What Is a Payoff and How Is It Different from Self-Sabotage?

Self-sabotage is visible in procrastination, perfectionism, or avoidance. A payoff, on the other hand, is more subtle. It's the internal reward we receive from maintaining a limiting pattern. While self-sabotage looks like resistance, a payoff feels like protection.

It protects us from discomfort, but often at the cost of growth.

Four Common Emotional Payoffs

Let's break down the most common types of payoffs we unconsciously cling to:

1. Avoiding the Unknown

The payoff: The illusion of safety.

Change means stepping into uncertainty. But uncertainty is uncomfortable, and the brain is wired to seek familiarity even if it's painful.

Example: You stay in a draining job because the idea of changing careers feels terrifying. The misery is familiar and therefore feels safer than the unpredictability of joy.

As Tony Robbins says: *"We change when the pain of staying the same becomes greater than the pain of change."*

2. Avoiding Judgment

The payoff: Protection from criticism or rejection.

Authenticity requires vulnerability, and vulnerability invites judgment. The fear of "being seen" is real, especially if past experiences have taught you it isn't safe.

Example: You don't speak up in meetings, afraid your ideas won't be good enough. You crave recognition, but the fear of embarrassment is stronger. Staying invisible feels safer until the cost of staying small becomes unbearable.

3. Avoiding Failure

The payoff: Avoiding shame or disappointment.

The fear of failure can be so intense that we avoid trying altogether. It's not that we're unmotivated; it's that the emotional risk feels too high.

Example: You want to start a business, but keep "endlessly researching" instead of acting. You're not lazy, you're scared. Failing feels more threatening than the low-grade dissatisfaction of never starting.

4. Avoiding Success

The payoff: Escape from pressure, expectations, and the fear of not being able to maintain it.

Believe it or not, success can be just as scary as failure. With success often comes responsibility, visibility, and higher stakes.

Example: You earn a promotion but start to self-sabotage. Why? Because success feels heavy. It demands more of you. A part of you may question whether you're truly worthy of it. Staying small feels safer, even if it limits your growth.

All of these payoffs have one thing in common: protection.

They protect you from perceived threats, judgment, change, pain, and shame. But they also block you from fulfillment. The key to transformation is understanding that the desire to grow and the desire to stay safe can exist at the same time. Once we recognize this, we gain the power to choose consciously.

A Personal Reflection

In my twenties, I held a lot of anger and hurt about the nature of my relationship with my dad. He wasn't emotionally available, and I often felt he was critical of me and the path I was taking in life. For a long time, I blamed him for a lot of things.

What I didn't realize at the time was that I was the one suffering from holding onto that anger. I wasn't aware of it when I first encountered the concept of a payoff, but eventually, I began to examine what I was getting out of staying in that emotional loop.

And the truth was: it allowed me to stay the same. It allowed me to remain in pain, to tell the story of how hard things were for me, to receive attention even if it was rooted in sympathy or drama.

That was my payoff.

The moment I saw that clearly, everything changed. I began doing the work to rewrite my story, not out of denial, but from a place of reclaiming my power. I chose to release the narrative that kept me stagnant, and with that decision, healing became possible. I now have a great relationship with my dad because I am authentically myself and don't try to people-please him anymore.

Reflective Shifts: Moving Beyond the Payoffs

For each payoff, here's a practice and a few reflection questions to help you begin the shift:

Avoiding the Unknown

Try: Take a small, unfamiliar step. Notice the emotions that arise: curiosity, fear, and anticipation.

Ask:

What am I afraid will happen if I change?

Can I sit with uncertainty and still move forward?

Avoiding Judgment

Try: Share one idea or opinion today, even if your voice shakes.

Ask:

What am I protecting by staying quiet?

What might I gain by letting myself be seen?

Avoiding Failure

Try: Take one manageable risk. Track what happens, not just the outcome, but how it feels internally.

Ask:

What story am I telling myself about failure?

What would I do if I believed failure led to growth?

Avoiding Success

Try: Break down a recent success into smaller steps. Ease into expansion one piece at a time.

Ask:

What fear lies beneath my success?

What would life feel like if I fully embraced it?

Compassionate Inquiry: Listening Instead of Forcing

Instead of bulldozing through resistance, compassionate inquiry invites us to listen to our inner protector with curiosity, not criticism.

Grab your journal and explore the following:

List three areas in your life where you feel stuck.

1. Ask yourself:

What do I gain by staying here?

What am I avoiding by staying in the familiar?

What illusion of safety am I clinging to?

2. Once you identify a fear, ask:

What is this fear trying to protect me from?

What belief am I holding beneath this reaction?

When you're ready to move forward, try this gentle affirmation:

"Hello, fear. Thank you for protecting me. I see you. I'm safe now. You can rest."

This respectful, compassionate approach can create more lasting transformation than force or pressure ever could.

A Personal Note on Rewriting My Payoffs

In my own journey, "playing small" was a hidden comfort I didn't realize I was holding onto. It kept me safe from judgment but also kept me invisible. It was a kind of internal bargain: *Stay quiet and you won't be rejected.*

Writing this book meant facing that emotional inertia head-on. I couldn't connect deeply with others or my own purpose until I was willing to stop hiding.

Feel the Fear and Do It Regardless

There was another time in my life when I was doing everything "right" to find a partner, dating, affirming, and even hosting events. Yet nothing was clicking. Frustrated, I went out with a friend one day and admitted how much I was struggling. She asked me something pivotal:

"What's on the other side of your desire?"

At first, I didn't understand. Then she added,

"Are you both excited and terrified?"

That cracked something open in me. I realized that the fear of being fully seen was coexisting with my deep desire to be loved. I had to feel both in order to move forward.

This is the duality of change: the coexistence of fear and longing. Ever since that moment, I've learned to hold fear alongside excitement as a natural part of stepping into the life I truly want.

Reframing: The First Step toward Lasting Change

Start with just one goal and reframe it from a place of fear or avoidance to one of aspiration.

- Instead of: "I want to lose weight."
- Try: "I want to feel light, energized, and vibrant in my body."

This subtle shift orients you toward growth, not lack.

Once your goal is clear, explore the hidden payoff:

- What am I getting from staying stuck?
- What might I gain by letting go?

Remember: Change isn't about pushing harder.

It's about listening deeper.

Ask yourself:

- What is the cost of staying the same?

- What might become possible if I released this payoff?

By honoring our fears and understanding their role, we reclaim the power to choose. Each small, brave act, each reframed story, builds the foundation for real, lasting transformation. Once we recognize the payoff, we can begin to question it and create a more empowering narrative. This is abracadabra at work again. What spell have you been casting?

Now that we've explored limiting patterns, self-sabotaging behaviors, and emotional payoffs, let's turn our attention to boundaries and uncover why they are essential for your well-being and authenticity.

Part 4

Living From the Inside Out

Chapter 10

Rediscovering Personal Power: Setting Boundaries

"Saying no to someone or something is, in fact, saying yes to ourselves."

The Threshold: Who You Were vs. Who You're Becoming

Many people tell me that boundaries feel "harsh." Even when they intellectually know boundaries are important, the guilt, fear, or people-pleasing tendencies make the process of setting or enforcing a boundary feel uncomfortable.

But boundaries aren't just rigid walls.

What Are Boundaries, Really?

Boundaries are the limits we set to protect our mental, emotional, and physical well-being. They define where we end and others begin, allowing us to navigate relationships and commitments in a way that honors our needs and values. A boundary is a flexible, supportive framework for protecting your energy and creating healthy connections. Each boundary becomes a protective spell, an energetic circle that safeguards your truth and honors your worth.

Boundaries are the natural outcome of "refocusing inward" and are essential for living authentically from the inside out. They mark the threshold between who we used to be: overextended, accommodating, burned out, and who we're becoming: anchored, clear, and strong.

If the first half of this journey has been about coming home to yourself, this chapter represents the moment you begin protecting that home with your choices, your voice, and your presence.

Setting boundaries isn't just about protecting ourselves. And they aren't barriers; they're pathways to deeper self-awareness and more fulfilling relationships. They are how we hone our own energy so we can become the magicians of our life.

The Default "Yes"

Imagine waking up already tired. The weight of a packed calendar presses on your chest before your feet even hit the floor. You scroll through messages and say "yes" to things you don't really want to do without thinking. Your "yes" is automatic, a reflex.

But what if you could press pause?

What if you could feel the difference between obligation and desire and choose from a place of alignment?

How often do you say "yes" out of habit or to please others, even when it drains your energy? What would it feel like to pause and reflect before committing?

The Body Knows

So, what do boundaries feel like?

Think about the tightness in your stomach when someone asks for a favor you don't want to give, but you say yes anyway. That discomfort is your body alerting you to a crossed boundary. The body often signals what the mind is unwilling to admit.

In this sense, boundaries are the sacred terms and conditions of your nervous system.

The Fear of Saying "No"

In third grade, I learned the hard way how scary it can feel to say "no." A classmate, Sara, bullied me when I stood up for myself on the playground. It was my turn on the swing, and I insisted on taking it. That small act of self-assertion was met with ridicule, and it planted a seed of fear that followed me for years.

Later in life, I began to recognize that fear. Saying "no" felt dangerous, not because it was, but because I was responding to an old pattern. Understanding that allowed me to loosen its grip. I learned that setting boundaries isn't inherently unsafe; it's a learned response rooted in past experience.

Saying "no" often triggers a fear of conflict, especially for those of us who were taught to avoid confrontation at all costs. But when we reframe conflict as an opportunity for growth, we start to see boundaries not as selfish acts but as acts of self-respect and empowerment.

Getting Curious About Your "Yes"

As you begin to observe these patterns in yourself, start questioning them:

- Why do I feel compelled to say "yes" when I want to say "no"?

- What am I afraid might happen if I disappoint someone?

- Am I afraid of judgment, rejection, or being seen as "difficult"?

- What would it look like to prioritize my own well-being, even if it means others might not approve?

Saying "No" Is Saying "Yes" to Yourself

A dear friend of mine, a former university dean turned successful writer, once shared a powerful insight: in her later years, she has come to enjoy saying "no." She told me she gets genuine pleasure from crossing things off her calendar. For her, it's no longer about being busy, it's about being intentional.

Saying "no" to someone else, she reminded me, is often saying "yes" to yourself. How empowering is that?

This resonated deeply with me. As a caretaker and someone who truly enjoys saying "yes" to life, I used to do so mindlessly. I took pride in my openness to new experiences and my willingness to help others.

But I didn't think twice about the cost. I would commit to too much in the name of joy or service until I burned out. I'd be superwoman for weeks, then crash for days.

It took time to recognize that constantly saying "yes" wasn't a badge of honor; it was a sign I wasn't listening to my own limits. Setting boundaries didn't mean I had to close off; it meant I had to get honest about what I had to give.

When Saying "Yes" Costs Too Much

I remember one Sunday night in particular. I was curled up on the couch, utterly depleted. My muscles ached from a week of tension I hadn't even noticed building. I'd said "yes" to three events back-to-back, and by the time I had a moment to myself, I wasn't even sure what I needed. I just knew I was running on empty.

That night, I realized something important: my "yes" was costing me too much.

Can you relate?

Where in your life are you saying "yes" when your body is saying "no"? What part of you fears rejection if you set a limit?

The First Brave "No"

I remember the first time I consciously and courageously said "no" to a request I would have agreed to in the past. It was something small, but I knew if I had committed with a yes, it would flatten me emotionally. My heart raced. My voice shook. I felt like I was doing something wrong.

But I said it anyway.

And when the world didn't fall apart and when the person on the other end actually respected my limit, I felt something unfamiliar rise in me. It wasn't pride, exactly. It was relief. For once, I hadn't betrayed myself.

That's the thing about boundaries: at first, they feel unnatural, especially if we're used to earning love through over giving. But over time, they become the most honest form of care we can offer ourselves and others.

"Me Time" Is Not Selfish

These days, I schedule "me time" into my calendar as a reminder to prioritize myself. This balance between showing up for others and nourishing my own energy is key to avoiding burnout. And yes, even for us extroverts, this matters.

Surprisingly, I've found that I can show up more fully for others when I honor my boundaries. I'm not giving from a place of depletion. My "yes" has weight because it's not diluted by resentment. And then my "no" isn't an apology, it's a recalibration.

Exploring the Boundaries That Matter to You

Let's explore the different types of boundaries you might want to reflect on and strengthen in your own life:

1. **Emotional Boundaries**

   Protect your emotional energy, avoid manipulation, and set limits around oversharing or emotional dumping.

2. **Physical Boundaries**

   Honor your need for personal space and communicate your physical comfort levels clearly.

3. **Time Boundaries**

   Manage how much time you give to others, including work, social commitments, and personal downtime.

4. **Digital Boundaries**

   Navigate screen time, social media use, and online interactions intentionally, especially in today's hyper-connected world.

Boundaries show up in all areas of life. Emotional boundaries help us say "no" to draining conversations or toxic dynamics. Time boundaries allow us to carve out space for self-care. Knowing which boundaries you need is the first step toward balance and inner peace.

A Closer Look at Physical Boundaries

Take physical boundaries, for example. Many people now work from home, thanks to digital technology. But without a clear separation between work and personal space, it's easy to feel overwhelmed. If your "office" is your living room, it can be hard to mentally "leave work" at the end of the day.

Setting up a desk in a separate room or designating a specific area you can physically step away from can help. Even a small, defined workspace can reduce anxiety and signal the end of the workday, creating a clearer boundary between work and home life.

Another aspect of physical boundaries involves how much space we need between ourselves and others to feel safe and comfortable.

I remember riding a crowded bus in India, shoulder to shoulder with strangers. I felt deeply uncomfortable, though I couldn't articulate why. Later, I realized it was because back home in Canada, we're used to much more personal space, especially in public settings. That experience showed me how unspoken and culturally shaped physical boundaries can be.

A different memory comes to mind from a work conference I attended a few years ago. I was talking with a project lead, an enthusiastic "close talker." He stood so close while speaking that I could smell his breath. I found myself leaning back subtly, trying to create space. His sense of physical boundaries was clearly different from mine.

If subtle cues like stepping back don't make someone aware of your discomfort, verbally expressing your boundary can be incredibly empowering. Unfortunately, boundary-setting isn't something most of us are taught, especially in Western culture. If I could add one thing to school curriculums (and believe me, I have a long list), it would be the importance of recognizing and communicating personal boundaries.

One of the most essential truths about boundaries is this: everyone's boundaries are different. A boundary that feels obvious to you might not be intuitive to someone else. This is especially important in relationships, be it romantic, professional, or platonic.

If you can't identify and express your own boundaries or listen to others express theirs, conflict and misunderstanding are almost inevitable.

Maintaining healthy boundaries doesn't mean you're being cold or distant. It simply means you're honoring your individuality, self-respect, and emotional well-being. I invite you to read that last part again.

Time Boundaries

Imagine a friend invites you to an impromptu get-together. Your first instinct may be to say "yes," whether out of habit, a desire to please, or genuine enthusiasm. But what if, instead, you paused to reflect on your energy and current commitments?

A simple response like, "I'd love to! Let me check my schedule and get back to you," creates breathing room. It allows you to assess your needs and make a decision from a place of alignment rather than obligation.

If you want to demonstrate integrity and build trust, consider adding a clear follow-up:

"I'll get back to you by this evening."

This not only respects your time, but it respects theirs too.

When you pause before committing, you give yourself the gift of presence. You protect your time and emotional resources while still being thoughtful and considerate.

One strategy I often recommend to clients is conducting a weekly review of their calendars. I ask them to identify any energy-draining activities and, if they can't eliminate them, to balance those obligations with things that rejuvenate and replenish them. This might include restorative yoga, spending time in nature, or simply enjoying a quiet night in.

By intentionally managing your schedule and setting boundaries around your time, you can reclaim your energy, reduce stress, and create a more sustainable, fulfilling rhythm in your life.

Take a moment to reflect:

- Are there activities or people in your week that consistently drain your energy?
- What small shifts could you make to balance them with something that refuels you?

Emotional Boundaries

Let's say you have a friend who frequently calls to vent, often without warning, and sometimes talks for hours. The phone buzzes again. It's her. You already know how the conversation will go: another hour of emotional unloading.

You care about her. Deeply. But your stomach clenches. You're tired. You've had a hard day. You want to be a good friend, but right now, you simply don't have the emotional bandwidth.

This is a moment when a boundary becomes an act of love, not rejection.

Protecting your emotional well-being is not selfish. It's necessary. In these moments, it's important to gently communicate your needs. You might say something like:

"I hear you, and I know this is important. But I'm feeling a bit overwhelmed right now. Could we check in with how we're both doing before diving into heavier stuff?"

This kind of response doesn't shut the person down. Instead, it models emotional awareness and reciprocity. It reminds them that emotional sharing is a two-way street, and it encourages both of you to show up more mindfully.

You can also set limits around time:

"I can talk for about 20 minutes today, I need to finish something afterward."

Small, clear, and compassionate statements like these help establish a pattern. Over time, they guide others to respect your emotional capacity without feeling pushed away.

Digital Boundaries

In a world where we are constantly connected, digital boundaries are essential for preserving our mental and emotional well-being. By mindfully managing your screen time, social media usage, and digital interactions, you protect your energy from information overload, negativity, and constant distraction. These boundaries give you the space to engage with technology intentionally, rather than allowing it to run your life.

Here are a few ways to establish healthier digital boundaries:

- **Digital Detox:** Create a "digital sunset," a set time each night when you disconnect from emails, social media, and screens. This simple boundary helps you unwind, sleep more restfully, and protect your emotional health.

- **Social Media Limits:** Ever find yourself scrolling late into the night, only to wake up feeling disconnected and drained? Try setting a daily time cap (like 20 minutes) or adopting screen-free Sundays. These intentional breaks can help you reclaim your attention and sense of purpose.

- **Notification Boundaries:** Constant pings and pop-ups can fragment your focus and overwhelm your nervous system. Consider turning off non-essential notifications or setting "Do Not Disturb" hours to create mental space and calm.

- **Offline Rituals:** Build habits that don't involve screens like journaling, walking, cooking, or reading. For example, I recently replaced my nightly scroll with a reading ritual before bed. That quiet time helps me wind down and end my day with peace, rather than digital noise.

Boundaries also apply to digital work life. If you work from home, setting limits around work emails, messages, and calls is vital for maintaining balance. Without clear boundaries, work can bleed into personal time, leading to stress and eventual burnout.

From Awareness to Practice: Boundaries in Daily Life

The first step in setting boundaries is cultivating awareness. As with any shift in behavior, awareness helps you spot patterns that aren't serving you.

Start paying attention to how you react to requests. What happens inside you when you say "yes" when you mean "no"? Do you feel physical tightness in your chest? A racing heartbeat? And what does your inner voice say in those moments? Is there fear? Guilt? People-pleasing? Ask yourself: Where did this voice come from? How long has it been with me?

Remember, setting boundaries isn't about pushing people away; it's about staying anchored in your truth so you can show up more fully for both yourself and others.

Boundaries are about how you manage your energy in every area of life, and while no one gets this perfect, it's in the practice of boundary-setting that you begin to live in alignment with what truly matters to you.

Knowing what a boundary is, is one thing. Knowing how to communicate it, especially when your voice shakes, your chest tightens, or your eyes well with tears, is another.

Finding the Words: Boundary-Setting Scripts

Here are some simple, respectful phrases to help you express a boundary. These are not scripts to memorize but starting points to guide you toward your own authentic voice.

Gentle, Clear "No's"

- "I won't be able to commit to that."

- "That's not going to work for me."

- "Thanks for thinking of me, but I'm going to pass."

You might feel the urge to over-explain, but I encourage you to pause and let your words land. Often, the person will respect your clarity more than you expect.

If someone pushes or persists, you can stay grounded with:

Compassionate Clarifiers

- "I care about you, but I don't have the capacity for this right now."

- "That sounds important. I just don't have the bandwidth at the moment."

Remember: saying "no" is not unkind. It's one of the most powerful ways to honor your energy and show up from a place of integrity rather than obligation or resentment.

Boundaries in Relationships

Family

Setting boundaries with family can be especially challenging because they know us well and often know exactly how to push our buttons.

For example, my brother is an expert in this area, and my relationship with my mom has taught me the importance of physical boundaries when emotions run high. Creating space for myself during emotional triggers has helped preserve the health of our relationship. Setting boundaries in family dynamics can feel painful, but they're ultimately an act of love for both of us. By setting limits, I honor my needs and theirs.

When you think about your family dynamics, are there relationships or situations that might require stronger boundaries for your emotional well-being? What would it look like to set those boundaries with compassion?

Friends & Work

A Client's Boundary Breakthrough

One of my clients learned how to set clearer boundaries around her work schedule after weeks of feeling drained. I remember when she first came to me tired, irritable, and full of self-doubt. On the surface, everything looked fine. But internally? She was unraveling.

It wasn't until she named the misalignment with a work client that we uncovered how she'd been overriding her own values just to avoid conflict. Here's what she shared after her breakthrough:

"After countless reflections on what was draining me, I ultimately handed in my notice with a mainstay client. While I love the work in theory, in practice, the misalignment of values with my direct report was becoming soul-crushing. Choosing to leave was scary, but it was best for my mental and emotional health as well as my career."

— *R. Waite*

Have you ever found yourself in a situation where a commitment or relationship didn't align with your values? What helped you recognize that misalignment, and how did you respond?

While this may seem like an extreme example, it underscores the importance of knowing what you need to maintain balance in your life. For some people, it's not one big thing; it's a pattern: too many energy-output activities and not enough energy-input ones.

If you don't have room to add anything nourishing in, what would it look like to remove one energy-draining commitment?

Boundaries and Negativity: Protecting Your Energy

We've all encountered people who dwell on the negative, what I affectionately call "Negative Nancys," or individuals who consistently drain our energy with complaints.

A friend of mine, recently retired, found himself back in the workforce at an auto parts store. During retirement, he had started embracing a more positive and peaceful outlook. But when he returned to work, he was quickly reminded how others' negativity could affect his mood.

One day, during lunch, a coworker interrupted him with a litany of complaints as she often did, dumping her frustrations on whoever would listen. My friend, recognizing the toll it was taking, calmly but firmly said:

"What you put out there comes back, and I am not enjoying this negativity."

He then excused himself.

She never complained to him again.

When he shared the story with me, I was reminded how powerful and necessary boundaries are for protecting our energy. His response was simple, direct, respectful, and it worked.

Think about the people in your life who tend to focus on the negative or vent excessively. How does their energy affect your well-being? What boundaries might you need to protect your peace?

And also, let's not forget the power of our own words and energy.

Thoughts and words shape our reality. When we focus on problems in any situation, we attract more problems. It becomes a self-fulfilling prophecy. But when we use our language with intention, when we speak life into our experiences, we activate our own kind of magic.

Abracadabra.

Boundaries as Love

Ultimately, boundaries are a powerful act of self-love. They protect our energy, honor our needs, and help us live authentically. Whether it's saying "no" to obligations, stepping away from toxic conversations, or creating space in relationships, boundaries allow us to reclaim our peace and foster healthier, more respectful connections.

By embracing boundaries, we affirm our self-worth and teach others to respect our needs. So, ask yourself: how would it feel to embrace boundaries not as protection, but as a way to love yourself deeply?

This was really hard for me to wrap my head around for a long time, the idea that having a boundary with someone was a form of love. But once you truly understand this, boundaries become easier, and you can start living your life more authentically and true to yourself. Every time we honor our own limits, we affirm our worth. The more we practice this, the more we teach ourselves and others to respect our needs, strengthening our sense of self-worth.

Integrity as a Boundary

Speaking of love, I want to invite you to think of integrity as it relates to the way you show up in your life. For a long time, I thought integrity meant that if I made a commitment, I had to follow through no matter what. Over time, I began to redefine integrity as having the intention to show up and follow through, and if I can plan ahead with some flexibility, then I am being integral to myself.

I now see integrity as a form of self-love and care, and an opportunity to honor my own boundaries. For example, if a friend I rarely get to connect with wants to set a time to get together, and I wholeheartedly want to do this too, I say:

"Absolutely, I would love to connect. Let's commit to connect on that day at that time. Do you mind if we check in the day before to see where we both are in terms of capacity, so we can decide together what our connection will look like?"

This approach allows room for flexibility. If all I have capacity for that day is a phone call, I am still committing to a connection with my friend while also showing love and care for myself. Every time you say yes to yourself, you whisper: *"I matter."*

In this new story, I live from the inside out. My body is my compass, and I feel the signals now. When I override them, I notice. When I honor them, I soften. I can now let someone down without abandoning myself.

In this story, I am allowed to rest and be misunderstood. I can pause before answering because I trust myself enough to set boundaries.

We Normalize What We Tolerate

In addition to the reflective questions offered throughout this chapter, another practical tool I recommend is the Boundary Mapping exercise:

1. On a piece of paper, draw a circle to represent yourself.
2. List the people, activities, or situations outside the circle that tend to drain your energy or violate your personal space.
3. Identify the type of boundary you need for each item, whether it's time, emotional, or physical.
4. Write down specific actions you can take to set those boundaries.

Once you've explored how boundaries work and how they can transform your life, I challenge you to take one small step toward setting a boundary today. Whether it's saying "no" to a request, limiting your screen time, or communicating your emotional needs, remember: each step you take is a powerful act of self-care and self-respect.

In learning to say no, we make space for a deeper yes, the kind that comes from truth, not fear. This is where we stop performing wellness and start living it. Not perfectly, mind you, but powerfully.

Imagine walking into your week with clarity, not dreading obligations, but choosing what you do intentionally. You say no, not out of coldness, but because you finally understand that your energy is sacred. That you are sacred.

Living from the inside out means bridging internal retuning with external expression. You are beginning to see what boundaries make possible. They are not walls; they are doors leading you back to yourself. This next phase is about living in alignment, not just talking about it.

Once we have explored our boundaries, we become attuned to the balance that arises in our internal energies as a sustainable way of being. Balance is the cornerstone of our well-being, and next, we'll delve deeper into how this concept plays a crucial role in cultivating an authentic and intentional existence.

Chapter 11

Finding Balance: The Art of Giving and Receiving

"By cultivating a more balanced approach to both giving and receiving, we can nurture deeper connections, experience greater fulfilment, and live a more harmonious and fulfilling life."

The Importance of Balance in Nature

A few summers ago, I found myself on a boat with friends, enjoying a brief respite from the anxieties of the COVID pandemic. This story takes place during one of the small windows when we were allowed to gather in groups. Naturally, once that became an option, many of us jumped at the opportunity. In my case, I went on a weekend boating trip with friends.

As we drifted across the lake, surrounded by the serenity of nature, I began to reflect on the concept of balance. The world around me felt eerily still, a quiet calm that stood in stark contrast to the frenetic energy that had defined the months before. The air was thick with silence, the kind you only experience when life pauses, broken only by the occasional rustle of leaves in the wind.

Yet, amidst this stillness, nature continued its rhythmic balance. Even though the world felt frozen in uncertainty, filled with palpable fear and highly charged emotions, the trees swayed in the wind, reaching for the sky. The water gently lapped at the shore, and I realized in that moment that despite global turmoil, nature remained unfazed. It reminded me of the value in creating a balanced life. Nature is often such a powerful teacher.

This observation sparked a parallel thought: our well-being, like the natural world, depends on a healthy exchange of energy. The act of breathing, taking in air and releasing it, mirrors this natural cycle of giving and receiving. It is our mechanism for staying present in the world.

Then I considered the human heart. It tirelessly pumps blood throughout the body, a constant cycle of giving and receiving. Can the heart function effectively without both processes? Of course not.

A Reflection on Giving and Receiving

The contrast between nature's steady balance and the chaos we were experiencing as a society created a stark juxtaposition. It forced me inward to reflect on the importance of balance in both giving and receiving in order to live a life of ease.

Just as plants exchange oxygen and carbon dioxide in a symbiotic relationship, allowing both to thrive, we, too, must learn to embrace both the giving and receiving of our energies. This natural balance teaches us about the harmony necessary for a fulfilling life.

In this spirit, I invite you to reflect on your own relationship with giving and receiving. Take a moment to find a piece of paper, give yourself some space, and think about the following:

- How do you relate to the act of giving and receiving?
- Are you comfortable receiving or asking for help, or does it feel unnatural to you?
- Do you tend to prioritize others' needs over your own?
- Do you feel uncomfortable receiving kindness or help from others?

Many of us struggle to receive, viewing it as a sign of weakness. However, the ability to receive is crucial for our well-being. It allows us to nourish ourselves, accept support, and experience the love that surrounds us. It also allows the giver to feel that their offering is truly received, which is a gift to them in return. I know we don't often think this way, but it's true!

Some of us over-give, leaving our own needs unmet, deflecting compliments, and refusing help, believing we must take care of everything ourselves. Others may receive easily but struggle with giving back. Both imbalances can create tension in our relationships and within ourselves.

Challenges of Giving and Receiving in a Society of Scarcity

Some people are reluctant to give, believing there isn't enough to go around. I've seen this mindset in friends and family members who hoard resources, even when they have more than enough. These are the people who don't tip at restaurants, never bring anything to dinner parties, and count every penny as if their life depends on it.

Are you the person who takes a bottle of wine to a party but brings the last few sips back home with you? If you struggle with being generous or have a fear around giving, consider these prompts:

- Can you recall a time when you received but felt reluctant to give? What underlying story fueled that feeling?
- How can you begin to be more open to giving?

Personal Stories and Lessons

My mom has friends (a couple) who are always nickel-and-diming, despite owning three houses and recently receiving a large inheritance. They won't spend money on themselves unless it's thrifted or free from Facebook Marketplace. They show up to parties with the cheapest bottle of wine, drink the nicer booze while there, and then take whatever is left of their own bottle back home. I think you get the idea.

This fear of scarcity is deeply ingrained in a society that values individual success over collective well-being. It's a mindset shaped by capitalism and competition, where we are taught to grab what we can and hold onto it tightly, rather than coexist with generosity and trust.

My grandparents also had a scarcity mindset. However, they grew up during wartime, when food and clothing were genuinely scarce. It wasn't a perceived scarcity, it was quite real. Even still, while I have compassion for how their experiences shaped them, they never updated their internal scripts, even after becoming financially comfortable later in life, when the world was much more stable.

These stories stay with us unless we choose to rewrite them. If we let fear win, we slip into a life of separateness, which can be lonely and isolating.

Questions for Reflection

- Do you ever feel fearful of scarcity or not having enough?
- How does this mindset affect your ability to give or receive?
- How has society influenced your beliefs about abundance and scarcity?
- Can you challenge these beliefs and adopt a more abundant mindset?

By creating a balance between giving and receiving, we can foster deeper connections and live more harmoniously. Imagine if we could all embrace both with grace, trusting that each is essential to our well-being. Much like the balance we see in nature, this shift could help us build a more sustainable and fulfilling world, both personally and collectively.

On Generosity

What if you don't have a lot of money? Well, to be honest, I hear this more from people who have more than enough. Money isn't the measure of generosity.

I grew up with a close friend, Crystal, who had very little, yet her generosity was boundless. Crystal's family lived on welfare, but she always shared what little she had with me.

In elementary school, Crystal and I would often go to the grocery store at lunchtime. With what little money she had, she would buy us potato wedges and always share with me. She taught me that generosity isn't about wealth, and she showed me that it is not about the size of what we give but about the spirit with which we give.

Similarly, during my travels, I met many people in poverty whose generosity was extraordinary. This was puzzling to me at first, but I realized that the impoverished people I met actually experienced scarcity and that connection and spirit were all they had. For me, this concept reinforced the idea that generosity is an attitude, not a financial status.

I invite you to reflect:

- Have you experienced generosity in ways that weren't about money?

- How does generosity feel to you, beyond material wealth?

- How can you shift your perspective on what it means to be generous?

- How do you express generosity in your life, and is it balanced with receiving?

The Law of Reciprocity: The Energy You Give Is the Energy You Receive

We often hear the phrase, "What you put out into the universe comes back to you." This is the Law of Reciprocity. While it may not always be immediate or obvious, the energy we expend, the love we give, and the kindness we extend inevitably return to us in unexpected ways. All we have to do is notice. It sounds simple, but it's not always easy.

For those who are used to focusing on problems, their perspective becomes skewed. And what happens when you focus on problems? More problems show up. The opposite is also true. Once you decide you want a red sports car, suddenly you notice red cars everywhere. It almost seems as if they've multiplied exponentially, but in reality, you've just started noticing them, you've chosen your field of view.

It's understandable that, with the chaos of the world around us, fear can step in and influence us to cling to things, especially if we aren't aware of what's happening. However, when we focus on scarcity, we attract more fear and lack. But when we embrace abundance, gratitude, and trust, we open ourselves to receive blessings.

Reflect:

- Have you experienced the Law of Reciprocity in your life?
- Are you focusing on scarcity or abundance in your life?

- How can you shift your mindset to invite more positivity into your life?

Doubt and fear often hinder our ability to embrace this truth fully. We may question our worthiness, allow self-doubt to creep in, or create excuses that block us from receiving abundance. However, giving and receiving are two sides of the same coin, and both are essential for our emotional and spiritual well-being.

By cultivating a more balanced approach to both giving and receiving, we can nurture deeper connections, experience greater fulfillment, and live a more harmonious life.

Breaking Free from the "Giving" Script: Challenging Societal Expectations

Many of the people I work with come into my practice feeling tired and burnt out. Interestingly, many of these people have also been conditioned to prioritize the needs of others over their own. This deeply ingrained behavior passed down through generations often leads to burnout and resentment. This is the martyr self-sabotage story at work again.

- Have you noticed this pattern of selflessness in your upbringing?
- How has it impacted your ability to receive or set boundaries?
- How can you shift your beliefs to value both your well-being and the well-being of others?

- What steps can you take to challenge the societal pressures that prioritize giving over receiving?

It's time to challenge this expectation. We need to empower ourselves and future generations to embrace both giving and receiving with balance. It's time to move beyond outdated scripts that value self-sacrifice over self-care. Personally, I discovered that I wasn't really allowing myself to receive, and when I did, it felt quite uncomfortable. I sat in this discomfort with the knowledge that receiving and giving are both essential to living a balanced life.

We must work on developing new narratives, ones that acknowledge there is enough of everything in the world. We need to trust that everything we put out, we ultimately receive back. This is the Law of Attraction. It is the law of energy. And we are all beings of energy.

More importantly, it's essential to check in with ourselves and be honest about how we are operating in the world. When we start to take full ownership of our lives, transformation becomes possible.

I've included some questions below to help unpack your relationship with giving and receiving. Think about how you engage with the world in different areas of your life, mentally, emotionally, physically, and spiritually. Are there areas where you feel out of balance?

If you want to get the most out of this exercise, I encourage you to write your answers down in a journal or on a blank piece of paper.

Exercise: Reflecting on Your Giving and Receiving

- **Mental:** How do you give and receive intellectually? Are you open to learning from others, or do you tend to give advice without taking it in yourself?

- **Emotional:** How do you share your emotions with others? Do you allow yourself to receive emotional support, or do you prefer to keep things to yourself?

- **Physical:** In what ways do you take care of your body, and how do you allow others to support your well-being?

- **Spiritual:** How do you give and receive spiritually? Are you open to receiving support on your spiritual journey, or do you try to go it alone?

Take a moment to reflect on these questions and explore where you might create more balance. By reframing our understanding of giving and receiving, we can nurture deeper connections, experience greater fulfillment, and live a more harmonious life.

Having explored the concept of balance and its importance in how we embody living from the inside out, let's now focus on how we can achieve better balance in our friendships and romantic relationships. When we honor both giving and receiving, we step into energetic harmony, the kind of sacred balance that allows our inner magic to flow freely. When we find this equilibrium, we unlock inner peace, allowing us to navigate life with greater clarity, purpose, and fulfillment.

Chapter 12

Reclaiming Your Energy:
Navigating the Rhythms of Relationships

"True liberation lies in cultivating authentic and
Reciprocal relationships that nourishes the soul."

Identifying Energy Leaks in Relationships

Before we can build nourishing relationships, we must first understand what drains us and why we allow it. Healthy relationships require a delicate balance of giving and receiving, much like a thriving ecosystem. When one person consistently gives more than they receive, an imbalance forms, straining the foundation of the relationship.

That may sound obvious, but how often do we actually take the time to examine the flow of give and receive in our relationships? Many of us were taught that love means endurance, that if we just give more, hold more, carry more, things will eventually work out. But that belief is exactly what depletes us.

Brené Brown illustrates this insightfully in *The Gifts of Imperfection* (2010), where she shares that in her marriage, balance isn't about a strict 50/50 split. Instead, she and her husband regularly check in with each other to assess their "capacity," expressed in percentages. If one of them is operating at 20% on a given day, the other might take on 80%, provided they have the capacity to do so. It's this ongoing awareness and recalibration that keeps their relationship balanced.

This concept has been pivotal in my own life. My partner and I have started to adopt a similar practice of checking in before making decisions or requests. It's a small shift, but it changes everything, allowing us to approach each other with compassion rather than assumption.

I remember a day when my partner, who runs a busy solar energy business, called me, sounding overwhelmed. He typically functions well under pressure, so I didn't think much of it. We chatted for a bit, and then I asked if he could help clean the house over the weekend.

His response surprised me.

"That request feels heavy," he said, his voice tight with exhaustion.

I felt a surge of frustration. "But it's important," I replied. "I don't want to clean the whole house by myself."

When he clarified that he was operating at 10%, something shifted. I had assumed he had more to give simply because he sounded okay. That moment helped me see how critical it is to check in, not just assume. I had unknowingly added to his stress by overlooking his emotional state.

This wasn't just about chores. It was about awareness of his nervous system, his emotional load, and his capacity to receive a request in that moment. It made me reflect on how often we push our needs onto others without first attuning to the space they're in.

That interaction was a wake-up call. It helped me identify an energy leak in our dynamic: the habit of making requests without first creating emotional safety.

Understanding Nervous System Imprints

When we talk about capacity and balance in relationships, it's not just logistical, it's physiological. Our nervous systems hold onto imprints from the past, especially from childhood, shaping how we engage, give, receive, and protect ourselves in relationships.

For a long time, I stayed in relationships that were out of alignment. I prioritized my partner's needs, often suppressing my own. I carried a pattern rooted in early experiences, one where I unconsciously tried to "earn" love by giving more than I had to offer.

It wasn't until I reached emotional exhaustion in one relationship that I finally saw the imprint clearly. My most recent ex was a kind person, but his capacity to look beyond himself was limited. I kept waiting for him to "come around," to see my needs, to meet me where I was.

I rationalized everything: "He just needs time. He's overwhelmed. If I show him enough love and patience, he'll get there."

But beneath that rationale was a deeper imprint; one formed in childhood around not feeling emotionally met or understood by my father. I was reenacting the same dynamic, hoping for a different outcome. It wasn't just the relationship that drained me; it was the story beneath it. A story that said: *If I give enough, I will be loved.*

That realization didn't come easily. It came through emotional exhaustion, through listening to the ache in my body, and through the painful clarity that this dynamic wasn't sustainable or balanced.

Eventually, I made the choice to walk away, not out of anger, but out of deep respect for myself. I understood that by staying, I was reinforcing the story that I had to earn love. Choosing to leave wasn't just a breakup; it was a nervous system revolution. For the first time, I stopped abandoning myself. It was a turning point toward living from the inside out.

From that place of honesty and self-respect, something beautiful unfolded. I broke the cycle of my own relationship patterns and I created space. And six months later, I met my life partner. The difference was immediate and undeniable; I didn't have to perform, shape shift, or wait for him to "see me." He already did. He pursued me. There was no second-guessing, and I just knew.

This is the power of understanding our nervous system imprints. When we bring awareness to our default relational patterns, often wired in through early experiences, we gain the ability to choose differently. We can regulate, pause, and course-correct instead of reacting from old wounds.

I still have moments where I go into old stories or abandon my own needs, but again, this work takes practice. And practice makes more permanent, not perfect.

Reclaiming and Embodying Balance in Relationships

One of the most transformative steps I took towards practicing more permanence was anchoring new ways of being through tangible rituals. For instance, I bought a ring as a symbolic reminder of my commitment to myself. It represents my "why," my purpose to be of service to others, while honoring the truth that I can't serve sustainably if I'm burned out or misaligned. Symbolic rituals help root us in a new identity, one that prioritizes balance, alignment, and truth over people-pleasing.

This anchoring practice helped me embody balance, not just think about it. It reminded me that self-care is foundational to every interaction I have with others and with myself.

Love languages were another powerful awareness tool that helped me create balance in both friendships and romantic relationships. When we understand how we and our loved ones give and receive love, whether through words, time, acts of service, gifts, or touch, we reduce miscommunication and the pain of unmet needs.

I've had relationships where I felt unseen, only to realize later that my friend or partner was expressing love through acts of service, fixing things, handling logistics while I was waiting for words of affirmation and quality time. Once I recognized the mismatch, I could appreciate their gestures more deeply and communicate my needs more clearly.

This kind of clarity fosters emotional safety, the real foundation of thriving relationships. When we feel safe physically, emotionally, and energetically, we can bring our full selves forward without fear of judgment or rejection.

But emotional safety requires honesty. And honesty sometimes means having hard conversations.

One friendship taught me this in a big way.

Friendship Imbalances

Catherine was fun and generous on the surface. But over time, I realized her generosity came with strings. She didn't listen deeply. Conversations always circled back to her. I gave more than I received, and I began to feel drained.

Eventually, I found the courage to name it. I told her I wanted more mutuality, more presence, more emotional reciprocity. I spoke with love, not blame.

Her response? She blocked me and everyone else in our circle.

It hurt. But it also clarified everything. I had honored my truth. And in doing so, I created space for more aligned relationships, ones where I feel seen, supported, and energized.

Being honest with someone, especially when it feels uncomfortable, is difficult. It can stir up the fear of rejection. But if we avoid honesty, we rob others of the opportunity to grow and understand how their behavior affects the world around them. I won't pretend it's easy; it takes courage, but it is so worth it.

Inviting growth by releasing draining friendships or "situationships" creates space—a sacred void for relationships that replenish us in more nurturing ways. Breaking free from imbalanced dynamics can be painful, but it's a crucial step toward cultivating deeper, more fulfilling connections.

A Simple Exercise to Assess Your Friendships

So, how do we start doing this? Here are a few journaling prompts to consider:

- "Where in your relationships do you feel drained rather than energized?"
- "What roles are you unconsciously playing to feel safe or needed?"
- "What does your body feel like around people who nourish you versus those who deplete you?"

As you begin responding to these questions, I invite you to pay attention to what happens in your body when you are relating to another person. This is what I call a somatic check-in. Where do you feel tight or tense? What is your body trying to tell you? Take time to really listen and be honest with yourself about how you're feeling in certain relationships.

Mapping Your Relationships: Visualizing the Flow of Energy

To gain clarity on your relationships, try creating a visual map of your energy flow. This simple exercise helps you assess where your energy is going and whether your connections feel balanced or draining.

Here's how to do it:

Draw Your Circle

1. Grab a piece of paper and draw a large circle in the center. This circle represents you and the core of your energy.

Add Your Relationships

2. Around your circle, draw smaller circles to represent the important people in your life. These might include friends, family members, coworkers, or anyone you engage with regularly.

Map the Energy Flow

3. Think about how energy flows in each of these relationships. Use arrows to show the direction and balance of that energy:

    o An arrow pointing out from you indicates you're giving more than you're receiving.

    o An arrow pointing in toward you shows that you're receiving more than you're giving.

    o Bidirectional arrows represent mutual exchange and a balanced relationship.

Reflect on the Patterns

4. Step back and look at your map. Are there more arrows pointing away from you than toward you? Are some relationships consistently draining? Which ones feel fulfilling?

This exercise can be revealing. It shows you where your energy is going and where adjustments might be needed. Ideally, your relationships should have arrows pointing both ways, a mutual exchange of energy and support.

Use this awareness to set healthier boundaries, communicate your needs more clearly, and prioritize relationships that nourish you. It's a deceptively simple but powerful tool.

The Sacred Void

Letting go of outdated patterns, misaligned relationships, or limiting beliefs creates what I call a sacred void. It's the uncomfortable in-between space that opens up before something new and aligned can emerge. The theme of creating space has come up many times now throughout this book, and I hope you are starting to get that this is where the magic lies, *the pause. The potential. The sacred void.*

One of my clients experienced magic in the sacred void as follows: she was seeking a romantic partnership, but what she ultimately found was herself. Through our work, she let go of draining dynamics and casual connections that were blocking her from deeper intimacy. It was challenging and painful, but it created space for something more meaningful. A year later, after embracing the sacred void in her life, she sent me a message: **"It works. It worked. I found my partner, and he is exactly what I was hoping for."**

This is what alignment looks like, not a fantasy, but a grounded reality born from truth-telling, self-trust, and spaciousness.

When we become aware of our nervous system patterns, honor our needs and capacities, and set boundaries rooted in self-respect, everything begins to shift. We don't just hope for better relationships, we create them.

When we allow what no longer serves us to fall away, we create space for something more authentic to emerge. And that space is not loneliness; it's sacred preparation.

Cord Cutting: Letting Go of What No Longer Serves You

Now that you've mapped your relationships, it's time to take meaningful action. One powerful way to free yourself from draining dynamics is through a practice called cord cutting. This exercise helps you release unhealthy attachments and energetic ties that are no longer aligned with your growth.

Here's how to do it:

1. **Find a Quiet Space**

Sit in a comfortable spot where you won't be disturbed. Close your eyes and take a few deep breaths to center yourself.

2. Visualize the Person or Situation

Bring to mind the person or situation you want to release. This could be a friend, partner, or any relationship that feels energetically heavy or depleting.

3. See the Cord

Imagine an invisible cord or string connecting you to that person. This represents the energetic tie between you.

4. Cut the Cord

Visualize yourself cutting that cord using scissors, a knife, or any tool that feels right to you. As you do this, feel the energy releasing from your body. This is your opportunity to let go of what's been weighing you down.

5. Send Healing Energy

After cutting the cord, send healing energy to both yourself and the other person. You are releasing the drain, not the love. You're choosing peace, clarity, and space for new, aligned connections to enter.

6. Affirm Your Boundary

Repeat to yourself:

"I am free from this energy tie. I create space for balanced, nourishing relationships."

Let the affirmation settle into your body and feel its power take root.

Cord-cutting can be a powerful and liberating ritual. It allows you to energetically detach from people, patterns, or unresolved emotions that no longer support your well-being.

Closing Affirmation

You are not here to be a vessel for other people's comfort. You are here to honor your energy, your body, your needs, and your truth.

When you do, the right people will rise to meet you.

You begin to attract relationships built on mutuality, respect, and depth, not because you demanded them, but because you became the version of yourself who no longer tolerates anything less.

This is the sacred art of energetic alignment.

This is how we reclaim our power.

This is how we live from the inside out.

Now, let's bring everything together in the next chapter and review how we can allow ourselves to step into a life guided by radical renewal, alignment, and embodied truth.

Chapter 13

Living From the Inside Out: Pulling it All Together

"When we are deeply connected to our values and authentically express ourselves, we attract experiences that align with our deepest desires."

During a longer term stay in Mexico a few years ago, as my relationship at the time was unraveling, I fully embraced the idea of living from the inside out.

Up to this point, I had done significant inner work, from healing past traumas to recognizing subconscious habits, and confronting patterns of control, people-pleasing, and self-sabotage. But in Mexico, I slowed down enough to really listen to myself. Through journaling, meditation, and mindful movement, I learned to meet my anxiety with compassion instead of judgment.

From that inner stillness, clarity began to emerge.

As my relationship ended, I asked myself three questions:

If this life isn't what I want, then what is?

If I'm breaking old patterns, what new stories and habits do I want to create?

What are my core values, and how do I align with them?

Three words rose clearly: Community. Connection. Contribution. These values had always been present, but I hadn't fully prioritized them. Starting to prioritize them was my turning point.

When I returned home, I began living intentionally through these values. I hosted community music jams, co-facilitated conscious connection workshops, and created spaces for people to share their stories, heal through sound and movement, and be witnessed with compassion. Every decision I made, I asked: Does this reflect my values, or is it a distraction?

I rekindled my love of writing, launched a coaching practice, and released music that felt true to me. These pursuits filled me with purpose and joy. For the first time, I wasn't operating from fear or autopilot anymore. My actions reflected my values. I was rooted in connection, contributing to others, and surrounded by a sense of community. I was beginning to live in alignment.

This shift wasn't about perfection or proving myself; it was about authenticity. I finally understood that fulfillment doesn't come from chasing external validation or operating on my default programming. It comes from aligning with what matters most and letting that guide every action. This alignment has reshaped my work and my purpose.

Honestly, I once believed changing the world meant starting an NGO or single-handedly striving for world peace. Now I see real change begins within. It starts with finding inner peace and radiating that outward, co-creating with others to spark a ripple effect. And right now, that approach is needed more than ever. With the chaos of political, environmental, and social tensions around the globe, this is how we can make a meaningful impact.

When our actions reflect our values, we naturally attract relationships, opportunities, and experiences that support our highest good. This leads to inner peace and fulfillment, which in turn expands our ability to serve and love others more deeply. I believe this is how we can change ourselves, our communities, and the world around us, for the better.

I now keep a sticky note on my altar that reads:

It is my responsibility to share my work with the world.

Whenever I feel afraid of being seen, worry that I'm too much, or struggle with impostor syndrome, I look at that note. I've realized that my purpose is to *"spread magic so that we can all fly together."* This is my anchor to my bigger why and it reminds me of something essential: like all of you reading this, I have a unique spark of light meant to be shared. Every time I help someone reconnect to their truth and rediscover their light, my own sense of meaning deepens.

I've realized that even if my words or presence make a difference to one person, my life has been worthwhile. In a world where anxiety, loneliness, and disconnection are common, what greater gift can we give than to live in a way that fosters connection and compassion for ourselves, and for each other? This is how I plan to leave the world better than I found it.

The Invitation

"The power to change the world begins within each of us with the conscious decision to live differently and on our own terms."

Living from the inside out isn't about fixing yourself; it's about remembering who you are. It's about slowing down enough to hear your truth and choosing alignment, even when it's uncomfortable. It starts with curiosity. It continues with courage.

Ask yourself:

What are my core values, and am I living them daily?

Where am I still operating from fear rather than trust?

What would shift if I chose authenticity, even when my voice shakes?

How can I create more connection with myself, my community, and the world?

So, What's Next?

If you've made it to this page, chances are something inside you is stirring; a longing for a life with more purpose, depth, and meaning. A desire to feel more like you.

You deserve to speak your truth, take up space, and express yourself fully. Your voice, your vision, your energy matter. There is no one else with your exact essence, and the world is better when you show up as you.

So, if you're ready to step into a new way of being, I invite you to join me. Reach out for coaching, gather with others who are seeking growth, ask deeper questions, attend events that spark something in you. Because you're not alone. Having support through community, mentorship, and reflection, can change everything. Magic unfolds when you stay open and curious.

"Our deepest fear is not that we are inadequate.

Our deepest fear is that we are powerful beyond measure.

It is our light, not our darkness,

That most frightens us."

— Marianne Williamson

Last Reflections

As I look back on my own journey through heartbreak, healing, and coming home to myself, I remember the quiet mornings with my hand over my heart, asking, "What do I truly want?" I remember the ocean breeze in Mexico carrying away old versions of me. I remember the tears that marked turning points, and the stillness that came when I chose to listen instead of perform.

Living from the inside out is a way of being.

It's the radical, gentle act of slowing down long enough to hear your truth.

It's choosing alignment, even when your voice shakes.

It's dancing barefoot in your living room.

It's trembling as you speak your truth anyway.

It's trusting that clarity comes not from forcing, but from feeling.

I know now, deep in my bones: when you choose to live from the inside out, you stop chasing life and start creating it.

You become the author of your reality.

The anchor of your truth.

The catalyst for a more honest, awakened world.

This is how we shift the collective.

The power to change your life, and by extension, the world, begins with one choice. One breath. One moment.

And that moment... is now.

Because if not now, then when?

You've always held the wand.

And the spell? It's yours to cast.

The magic lives within you.

So go ahead—use it.

ABRACADABRA.

References

1. Twenge, J. M. (2017). *Has the smartphone destroyed a generation?* The Atlantic. https://www.theatlantic.com/magazine/archive/2017/09/has-the-smartphone-destroyed-a-generation/534198/

2. Orlowski, J. (Director). (2020). *The social dilemma* [Film]. Exposure Labs; Netflix.

3. Kishimi, I., & Koga, F. (2018). *The courage to be disliked: The Japanese philosophy that shows you how to change your life and achieve real happiness.* Atria Books.

4. Jeffers, S. (2007). *Feel the fear and do it anyway.* Ballantine Books.

5. Lerner, H. (2004). *The dance of fear: A woman's guide to changing the patterns of anxiety, worry, and fear.* Harlequin.

6. Hawkins, D. R. (2002). *Power vs. force: The hidden determinants of human behavior.* Hay House.

7. Aposhian, S. (2011). *The body talks: The healing power of listening.* CreateSpace Independent Publishing Platform.

8. Hay, L. L. (1999). *You can heal your life.* Hay House.

9. Kaehr, S. A. (2020). *Ancestral healing: Breaking the cycle of trauma and reclaiming your power.* Llewellyn Worldwide.

10. Mendelson, T. C., & McEwen, B. S. (2020). *Epigenetics and stress: Implications for mental health and disease. Psychiatry Research, 287,* 112935.

11. Duran, E. (2021). *The trauma of the gifted: How the seven generations principle can help us heal.* W.W. Norton & Company.

12. Truth and Reconciliation Commission of Canada. (2015). *Honouring the truth, reconciling for the future: Summary of the final report of the Truth and Reconciliation Commission of Canada.* Truth and Reconciliation Commission of Canada. https://www.trc.ca/

13. Keltner, D., Kogan, A., Piff, P. K., & Dacher, K. (2019). Social structure, power, and the regulation of emotion. In C. N. DeSteno (Ed.), *Handbook of social and emotional intelligence* (pp. 167–190). Springer.

14. Primack, B. A., Shensa, A., Sidani, J. L., Whaite, E. R., Lin, L., Rosen, D., Radovic, A., Colditz, J. B., Radunovich, H. L., & Miller, E. (2017). Social media use and perceived social isolation among young adults in the U.S. *American Journal of Preventive Medicine, 53*(1), 1-8. https://doi.org/10.1016/j.amepre.2017.01.010

15. Kabat-Zinn, J. (2003). Mindfulness-based stress reduction (MBSR). In *Mindfulness and health: A guide to stress reduction and emotional well-being* (pp. 69-93). Springer.

16. Zeidan, F., Johnson, S. K., Diamond, B. J., & David, Z. (2010). Mindfulness meditation improves cognition: Evidence of brief mental training. *Consciousness and Cognition, 19*(2), 597–605. https://doi.org/10.1016/j.concog.2010.03.014

17. Brach, T. (2020). *RAIN: A practice of radical compassion.* https://www.tarabrach.com/rain-practice-radical-compassion/

18. Sanguin, B. (n.d.). *CUBS: Creating a world of love, connection, and belonging.* BruceSanguin.ca. Retrieved February 11, 2025, from https://www.brucesanguin.ca

19. Robbins, T., Diamandis, P., & Hariri, R. (2022). *Life force: How new breakthroughs in precision medicine can transform the quality of your life & those you love.* Simon & Schuster.

20. Jung, C. G. (2017, September 15). *Top 5 payoffs of staying stuck. Psychology Today.* https://www.psychologytoday.com/us/blog/the-wise-open-mind/201709/top-5-payoffs-staying-stuck

21. Brown, B. (2010). *The gifts of imperfection: Let go of who you think you're supposed to be and embrace who you are.* Hazelden Publishing.

22. Chapman, G. (2015). *The 5 love languages: The secret to love that lasts* (5th ed.). Northfield Publishing.

23. Dziegielewski, S. F. (2013). *Social work practice with families: A resiliency-based approach* (3rd ed.). Springer Publishing Company.

www.ingramcontent.com/pod-product-compliance
Lightning Source LLC
Chambersburg PA
CBHW031525120626
46545CB00005B/2004